P · O · C · K · E · T · S
WEATHER FACTS

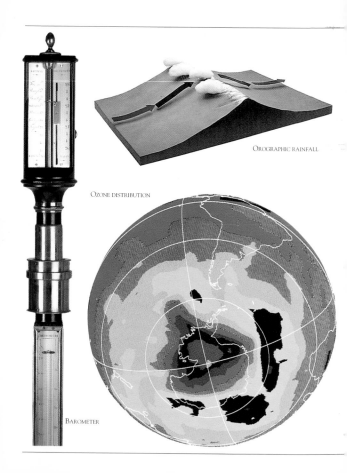

OROGRAPHIC RAINFALL

OZONE DISTRIBUTION

BAROMETER

P·O·C·K·E·T·S
WEATHER FACTS

Written by
PHILIP EDEN and
CLINT TWIST

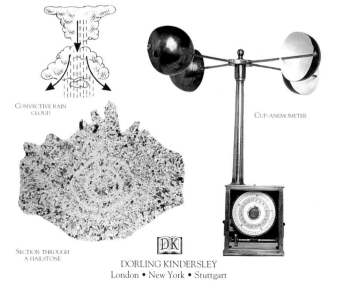

CONVECTIVE RAIN
CLOUD

CUP-ANEMOMETER

SECTION THROUGH
A HAILSTONE

DK

DORLING KINDERSLEY
London • New York • Stuttgart

A DORLING KINDERSLEY BOOK

Project editor	Clint Twist
Art editor	Alexandra Brown
Senior editor	Hazel Egerton
Senior art editor	Jacquie Gulliver
Editorial consultant	Philip Eden
Picture research	Fiona Watson
Production	Ruth Cobb
US editor	Jill Hamilton
US consultant	Dr. William A. Gutch
	Hayden Planetarium
	American Museum of Natural History

First American Edition, 1995
2 4 6 8 10 9 7 5 3 1
Published in the United States by
Dorling Kindersley Publishing, Inc.,
95 Madison Avenue
New York, New York 10016

Library of Congress Cataloguing-in-Publication Data
Eden, Philip
  Weather facts / written by Philip Eden and Clint Twist, - - 1st American ed.
     p.   cm. - - (Pockets)
  Includes index.
  Summary: Describes different weather conditions and how they are detected, discussing
climate, atmosphere, and storms.
  ISBN 0-7894-0218-1
  1. Weather - - Juvenile literature. 2. Meteorology - - Juvenile literature.
  [1.Weather. 2. Meteorology.] I. Title. II. Series
QC981.3.E34   1995
551.5 - - dc20   95-147
                                                                          CIP

Color reproduction by Colourscan, Singapore
Printed and bound in Italy by L.E.G.O.

CONTENTS

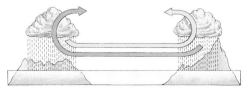

HOW TO USE THIS BOOK

These pages show you how to use *Pockets:Weather Facts*.
The book is divided into 13 sections. Each section
contains information on one aspect of weather.
At the beginning of each section there is a picture
page and a guide to the contents of that section.

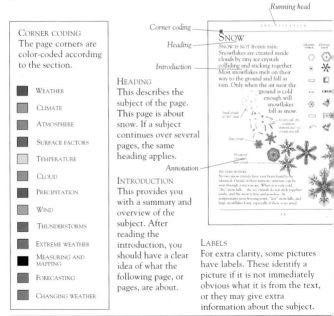

Running head

Corner coding

Heading

Introduction

Annotation

CORNER CODING
The page corners are
color-coded according
to the section.

WEATHER

CLIMATE

ATMOSPHERE

SURFACE FACTORS

TEMPERATURE

CLOUD

PRECIPITATION

WIND

THUNDERSTORMS

EXTREME WEATHER

MEASURING AND
MAPPING

FORECASTING

CHANGING WEATHER

HEADING
This describes the
subject of the page.
This page is about
snow. If a subject
continues over several
pages, the same
heading applies.

INTRODUCTION
This provides you
with a summary and
overview of the
subject. After
reading the
introduction, you
should have a clear
idea of what the
following page, or
pages, are about.

LABELS
For extra clarity, some pictures
have labels. These identify a
picture if it is not immediately
obvious what it is from the text,
or they may give extra
information about the subject.

RUNNING HEADS
These remind you which section you are in. The top of the left-hand page gives the section name. The right-hand page gives the subject. This page on snow is from the precipitation section.

DATA BOXES
Some pages have data boxes. These contain information in detail. In this case the box gives the meanings of some of the many words for "snow" in the Inuit language.

FACT BOXES
Many pages have fact boxes. These provide at-a-glance information about the subject, such as the average air pressure at sea level, or the fastest wind speed ever recorded.

Data box   *Fact box*

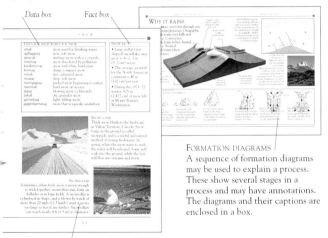

FORMATION DIAGRAMS
A sequence of formation diagrams may be used to explain a process. These show several stages in a process and may have annotations. The diagrams and their captions are enclosed in a box.

Caption

CAPTIONS AND ANNOTATIONS
Each illustration is accompanied by a caption. Annotations, in *italics*, point out the features of an illustration or diagram and usually have leader lines.

INDEX AND GLOSSARY
At the back of the book is an index listing every subject in the book. By referring to the index, information on particular topics can be found quickly. A glossary defines the technical terms used in the book.

WEATHER

WHAT IS WEATHER?

PLANET EARTH IS surrounded by an atmosphere of life-supporting gases. Weather is the state of the lower atmosphere at any particular time and place. People experience weather chiefly in terms of sunshine, snow, rain, clouds, and wind. These five products of the global weather-machine have enormous influence over styles of housing, clothing, food, and transportation.

CLOUDS
Most of the atmosphere's water is present in the form of invisible water vapor. Clouds store the atmosphere's surplus water in the form of tiny particles of water and ice.

EARTH
Photographed from space, our planet Earth looks like a shining blue jewel.

RAIN
When cloud particles become too heavy, they fall as rain, snow, or hail. This process (which is called precipitation) distributes freshwater over the Earth's surface.

SUNSHINE
Solar energy reaches the Earth mostly as heat and light. The Sun's heat energy drives the global weather-machine.

WIND
Heard and felt, but never seen, wind is the result of air moving as it circulates in both local and global patterns.

WEATHER AND SEASONS

IN SOME PARTS OF THE WORLD, weather is seasonal; it changes according to the time of year. Seasons depend on varying amounts of sunlight reaching different parts of the Earth's surface. These variations are the result of the Earth's orbit around the Sun on a tilted axis. In general, seasons become more noticeable with increasing distance from the equator.

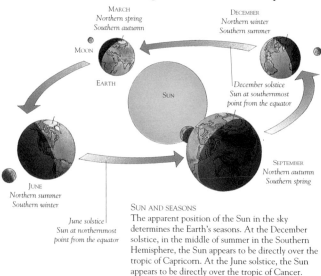

MARCH
Northern spring
Southern autumn

DECEMBER
Northern winter
Southern summer

MOON

EARTH

SUN

December solstice
Sun at southernmost
point from the equator

SEPTEMBER
Northern autumn
Southern spring

JUNE
Northern summer
Southern winter

June solstice
Sun at northernmost
point from the equator

SUN AND SEASONS
The apparent position of the Sun in the sky determines the Earth's seasons. At the December solstice, in the middle of summer in the Southern Hemisphere, the Sun appears to be directly over the tropic of Capricorn. At the June solstice, the Sun appears to be directly over the tropic of Cancer.

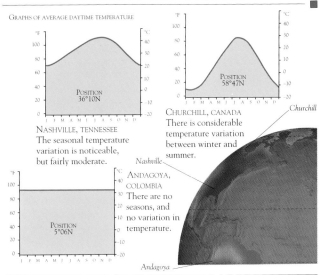

GRAPHS OF AVERAGE DAYTIME TEMPERATURE

POSITION
36°10N

NASHVILLE, TENNESSEE
The seasonal temperature
variation is noticeable,
but fairly moderate.

POSITION
58°47N

CHURCHILL, CANADA
There is considerable
temperature variation
between winter and
summer.

Churchill

Nashville

ANDAGOYA,
COLOMBIA
There are no
seasons, and
no variation in
temperature.

POSITION
5°06N

Andagoya

DATA: SEASONS AND DAYLIGHT (HOURS AND MINUTES)			
Date	Andagoya	Nashville	Churchill
1/15	11:51	10:00	6:38
2/15	11:58	10:56	9:11
3/15	12:06	11:55	11:41
4/15	12:14	12:45	14:31
5/15	12:20	14:00	17:04
6/15	12:23	14:32	18:49
7/15	12:21	14:26	17:31
8/15	12:17	13:32	15:46
9/15	12:09	12:27	13:00
10/15	12:01	11:19	10:11
11/15	11:53	10:21	7:37
12/15	11:49	9:46	5:54

SOLSTICE FACTS

• The June solstice
(midsummer in the
Northern Hemisphere)
takes place around
June 21–22.

• The December
solstice (midwinter in
the Northern
Hemisphere) takes
place around
December 22–23.

WEATHER AND CLIMATE

CLIMATE IS A LONG-ESTABLISHED PATTERN of weather.
This pattern may vary, or it may remain the same
throughout the year. Climate
is usually defined in terms
of temperature and rainfall.

WORLD CLIMATES:
TEMPERATURE

ALWAYS HOT

HOT SUMMER
WARM WINTER

HOT SUMMER
MILD WINTER

WARM SUMMER
COLD WINTER

COOL SUMMER
COLD WINTER

ALWAYS
COLD

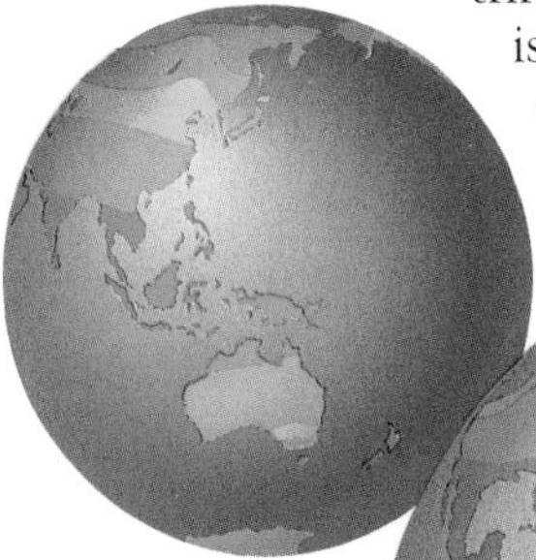

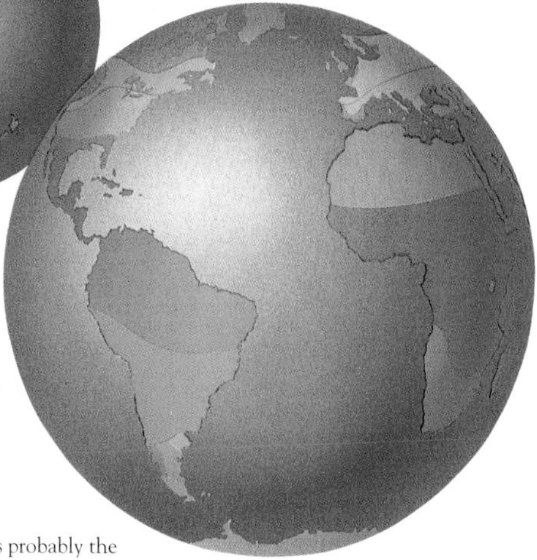

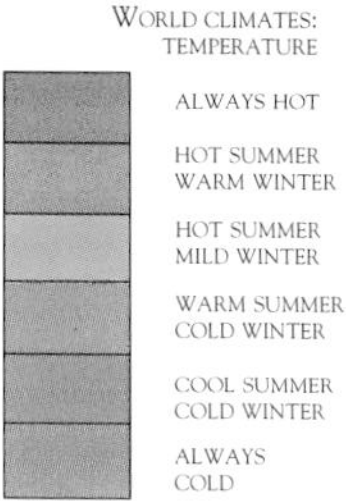

INFLUENCING CLIMATE

Geographical distance is probably the
main factor influencing the climate in any particular part
of the world. Distance from the equator affects temperature,
as does altitude (distance above sea level). Distance from a
coastline affects both temperature and rainfall, while distance
from a mountain range can increase or decrease rainfall.

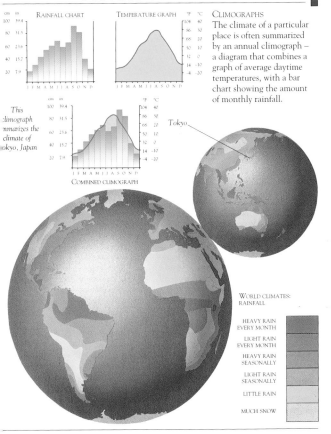

RAINFALL CHART

TEMPERATURE GRAPH

CLIMOGRAPHS
The climate of a particular place is often summarized by an annual climograph – a diagram that combines a graph of average daytime temperatures, with a bar chart showing the amount of monthly rainfall.

This climograph summarizes the climate of Tokyo, Japan

COMBINED CLIMOGRAPH

Tokyo

WORLD CLIMATES: RAINFALL

HEAVY RAIN EVERY MONTH

LIGHT RAIN EVERY MONTH

HEAVY RAIN SEASONALLY

LIGHT RAIN SEASONALLY

LITTLE RAIN

MUCH SNOW

CLIMATE

TROPICAL

YEAR-ROUND HIGH TEMPERATURES combined with
heavy rainfall are characteristic of a tropical climate.
Near the equator, the rainfall is distributed fairly
evenly throughout the year. Farther to the north and
south, the rainfall tends to be concentrated into a
distinct wet season. Altogether, about half of the
world's population live in regions of tropical climate.

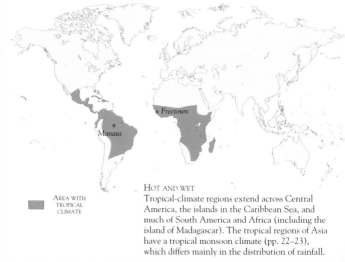

AREA WITH
TROPICAL
CLIMATE

HOT AND WET

Tropical-climate regions extend across Central
America, the islands in the Caribbean Sea, and
much of South America and Africa (including the
island of Madagascar). The tropical regions of Asia
have a tropical monsoon climate (pp. 22–23),
which differs mainly in the distribution of rainfall.

TROPICAL CONDITIONS
High temperatures, heavy rainfall, and lush vegetation make most tropical regions extremely humid (humidity measures the amount of water vapor in the air). Frequent rainfall means that the sky is often filled with clouds, and sunshine is fairly limited. In general, winds are light but tropical thunderstorms and cyclones (hurricanes) can cause considerable destruction.

LANDSCAPE
Tropical climates produce a characteristic natural vegetation known as tropical rainforest. The largest remaining rainforest is in the Amazon Basin, Brazil.

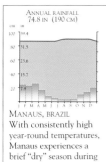

ANNUAL RAINFALL
74.8 IN (190 CM)

MANAUS, BRAZIL
With consistently high year-round temperatures, Manaus experiences a brief "dry" season during the months of July, August, and September.

ANNUAL RAINFALL
135.3 IN (343.6 CM)

FREETOWN, SIERRA LEONE
Situated on the coast, Freetown has six months of heavy rain each year. During the wet season, sunshine is limited to only 2–3 hours per day.

CLIMATE FACTS
• The kinetic energy of the raindrops in a tropical rainstorm is equivalent to 2,200 watts per acre (5,500 watts per hectare).

• In geography, the "Tropics" lie between the tropic of Cancer (23°30N) and the tropic of Capricorn (23°30S). Tropical climates extend beyond this strict geographical definition.

TROPICAL MONSOON

TORRENTIAL MONSOON rains dominate the climate in the tropical regions of Asia and Australasia. Twice a year, the prevailing winds reverse their direction completely. This shift in the wind divides the year into a rainy season followed by a predominantly dry season.

WET SEASON
In parts of India, the monsoon rains regularly produce flooding.

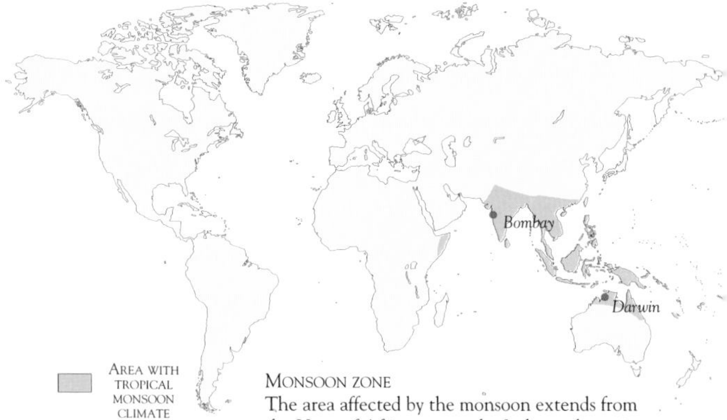

AREA WITH TROPICAL MONSOON CLIMATE

Bombay

Darwin

MONSOON ZONE
The area affected by the monsoon extends from the Horn of Africa, across the Indian subcontinent and Southeast Asia, to the northern coast of Australia. Seasonal monsoon-type weather also affects parts of Africa, and Central and South America.

NORTHEAST MONSOON
With the onset of winter (below), Central Asia becomes a high-pressure region, and the winds reverse direction. Cool dry winds blow from the northeast toward the equator, lowering temperatures.

SOUTHWEST MONSOON
During early summer (above), low pressure over Central Asia creates southwesterly winds that carry warm moisture-laden air from the Indian Ocean. These winds bring the heavy monsoon rains.

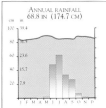

ANNUAL RAINFALL
68.8 IN (174.7 CM)

cm	in												
100	39.4												
80	31.5												
60	23.6												
40	15.7												
20	7.9												
		J	F	M	A	M	J	J	A	S	O	N	D

BOMBAY, INDIA
Nearly all of Bombay's rainfall occurs in the four months of the monsoon wet season – June, July, August, and September.

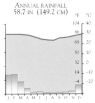

ANNUAL RAINFALL
58.7 IN (149.2 CM)

											°F	°C
											104	40
											86	30
											68	20
											50	10
											32	0
											14	-10
											-4	-20
J	F	M	A	M	J	J	A	S	O	N	D	

DARWIN, AUSTRALIA
Because it is situated south of the equator, Darwin has a dry season at the same time as Bombay has a wet season.

CLIMATE FACTS

• The word monsoon comes from the Arabic word *mausim*, which means "seasonal wind."

• Monsoon rains advance across Asia at a rate of about 60 miles (100 km) per day.

• At Cherrapungi in northern India, 864 in (22 m) of rain fell during the 1861 monsoon season.

DRY

LITTLE OR NO RAINFALL is the main characteristic
of the dry climate found in desert and semidesert
regions. Most deserts also experience high daytime
temperatures, but some are cool or even cold. The
large midlatitude deserts – the Sahara and Arabian
deserts – are the result of the global pattern of air
circulation. Dry air descends on these regions,
bringing clear skies and hot sunshine.

Kashgar

Timbuktu

AREA WITH
DRY CLIMATE

DRY ZONES
Regions of dry climate are found on every
continent except Europe. Some dry regions are the
result of global influences, while others result from
local factors. The west coast deserts of South
America and southern Africa are caused by cool
ocean currents flowing along the coast.

DRY CONDITIONS
Desert skies are usually cloudless with strong sunlight. Although the air above the desert surface heats up, it remains relatively cool compared with the ground. Sand or rocks in direct sunlight will easily reach 140–160°F (60–70°C). Dry air loses heat more quickly at night than moist air, so nighttime temperatures may drop to below freezing point.

LANDSCAPE
Large areas of the driest deserts are seas of sand dunes. The constantly shifting dunes prevent even the most drought-resistant plants from gaining a foothold.

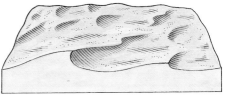

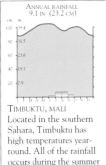

ANNUAL RAINFALL
9.1 IN (23.2 CM)

cm in
100 | 39.4
80 | 31.5
60 | 23.6
40 | 15.7
20 | 7.9

J F M A M J J A S O N D

TIMBUKTU, MALI
Located in the southern Sahara, Timbuktu has high temperatures year-round. All of the rainfall occurs during the summer months.

ANNUAL RAINFALL
3.4 IN (8.6 CM)

°F °C
104 | 40
86 | 30
68 | 20
50 | 10
32 | 0
14 | -10
-4 | -20

J F M A M J J A S O N D

KASHGAR, CHINA
Situated more than 1,000 miles (1,600 km) from the sea, Kashgar is hot in summer, cold in winter, and very dry throughout the year.

CLIMATE FACTS

• The world's driest place is the Atacama Desert in northern Chile. Between 1903 and 1917, the town of Arica received no rain at all for a period of 5,206 days.

• The sunniest place in the world is the town of Yuma, in Arizona, with an average of 4,127 hours of bright sunshine each year.

WARM

COMFORTABLE TEMPERATURES and moderate rainfall
throughout the year are found in warm-climate
regions. Some of these regions are described as
having a "Mediterranean" climate, but this term can
be misleading. Geographical conditions around the
Mediterranean Sea have created an especially mild
climate. Some warm-climate regions have more
extreme temperatures in both winter and summer.

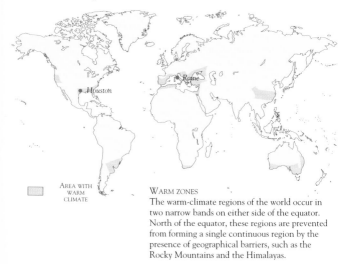

AREA WITH
WARM
CLIMATE

WARM ZONES
The warm-climate regions of the world occur in
two narrow bands on either side of the equator.
North of the equator, these regions are prevented
from forming a single continuous region by the
presence of geographical barriers, such as the
Rocky Mountains and the Himalayas.

WARM CONDITIONS

With mild winters and a long frost-free growing period, warm-climate regions are ideally suited to most types of agriculture. In California and the Mediterranean region, citrus fruits, grapes, and olives are important cash crops. In China, the warm-climate region is the most productive rice-growing area.

LANDSCAPE

Most of the natural vegetation has been cleared from warm-climate regions to make way for human settlements and agriculture.

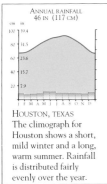

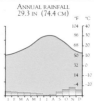

ANNUAL RAINFALL 46 IN (117 CM)	ANNUAL RAINFALL 29.3 IN (74.4 CM)

HOUSTON, TEXAS

The climograph for Houston shows a short, mild winter and a long, warm summer. Rainfall is distributed fairly evenly over the year.

ROME, ITALY

Situated slightly farther north, Rome has a shorter summer than Houston. Rainfall is more seasonal, and is highest during autumn.

CLIMATE FACTS

• A warm climate is no guarantee of a mild winter. In January 1932, 2 in (5 cm) of snow fell on Los Angeles, California.

• Europe's highest temperature of 123°F (50.5°C) was recorded in southern Portugal.

• The Mediterranean region has more than 30 individually named local winds.

COOL

COLD WINTERS with frequent nighttime frosts are characteristic of cool-climate regions. These regions have much more changeable weather than elsewhere. Cool-climate regions are strongly influenced by large moving weather systems called depressions, or "lows," and anticyclones, or "highs." As one of these systems passes over a particular location, it produces a series of changing weather conditions.

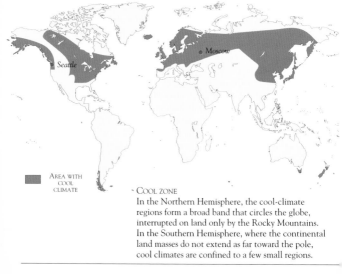

AREA WITH
COOL
CLIMATE

◦ COOL ZONE
In the Northern Hemisphere, the cool-climate regions form a broad band that circles the globe, interrupted on land only by the Rocky Mountains. In the Southern Hemisphere, where the continental land masses do not extend as far toward the pole, cool climates are confined to a few small regions.

COOL CONDITIONS
There is considerable variation across cool-climate regions because of their great geographical extent. Coastal regions often have a less extreme climate than regions farther inland. Deciduous trees, which lose their leaves in winter, are confined to the warmer regions. In general, human settlement and agriculture are similarly restricted by temperature.

LANDSCAPE
In most cool-climate regions, the landscape is still dominated by natural vegetation. Forests of needleleaf (coniferous) trees encircle the globe.

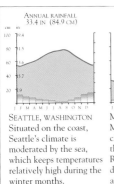

ANNUAL RAINFALL
33.4 IN (84.9 CM)

SEATTLE, WASHINGTON
Situated on the coast, Seattle's climate is moderated by the sea, which keeps temperatures relatively high during the winter months.

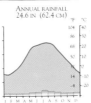

ANNUAL RAINFALL
24.6 IN (62.4 CM)

MOSCOW, RUSSIA
Moscow's inland climate is more extreme than that of Seattle. Rainfall also follows a different pattern, with a summer maximum.

CLIMATE FACTS
• The lowest recorded temperature in the Northern Hemisphere, –96°F (–71°C), was measured inside the cool-climate region at Oimyakon, Siberia.

• The highest recorded temperature in Britain is 98.8°F (37.1°C) in August 1990; and the lowest on record is –17.0°F (–27.2°C) in January 1982.

MOUNTAIN AND POLAR

MOUNTAINS CREATE THEIR OWN CLIMATE, no matter where they are located. The climate of a mountain or mountain range can be divided vertically into a number of subzones. While foothills may have a tropical climate, peaks may be covered in ice. Near the North and South Poles, the polar climate is dominated by low temperatures, strong winds, and year-round snow cover.

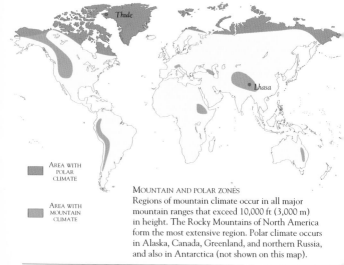

AREA WITH
POLAR
CLIMATE

AREA WITH
MOUNTAIN
CLIMATE

MOUNTAIN AND POLAR ZONES
Regions of mountain climate occur in all major mountain ranges that exceed 10,000 ft (3,000 m) in height. The Rocky Mountains of North America form the most extensive region. Polar climate occurs in Alaska, Canada, Greenland, and northern Russia, and also in Antarctica (not shown on this map).

MOUNTAIN CONDITIONS

The subzones of a mountain climate get progressively colder with increased altitude. The vegetation on the lower slopes largely depends upon which climate zone the mountain is in. On the upper slopes, needleleaf trees reach to the tree line. Above this level are found alpine plants which can withstand the harsh conditions. The uppermost level is bare rock and snow.

POLAR LANDSCAPE
Polar regions are dominated by snow and ice. Some parts of Antarctica are covered with a layer of ice more than 10,000 ft (3,000 m) thick.

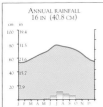

ANNUAL RAINFALL
16 IN (40.8 CM)

LHASA, TIBET
Situated some 12,000 ft (3,600 m) above sea level, Lhasa has surprisingly warm summers thanks to clear skies and strong sun.

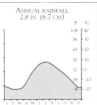

ANNUAL RAINFALL
2.6 IN (6.7 CM)

THULE, GREENLAND
Temperatures at Thule only rise above freezing during the middle of summer. The annual "rainfall" consists entirely of snow.

CLIMATE FACTS

• The highest recorded temperature inside the Arctic Circle is 100°F (37.8°C), at Fort Yukon, Alaska, in June 1915.

• The highest recorded Antarctic temperature is 58°F (14.4°C) in October 1958.

• Mount Kilimanjaro in Tanzania is the only permanent snowcap within sight of the equator.

ATMOSPHERE

WHAT IS THE ATMOSPHERE?

EARTH IS SURROUNDED by an atmosphere of gases about 500 miles (800 kilometers) deep. The gases are densest at the Earth's surface, and get progressively less dense with increasing height. The atmosphere shields the Earth from the harmful effects of solar radiation, and moderates the Earth's solar energy budget.

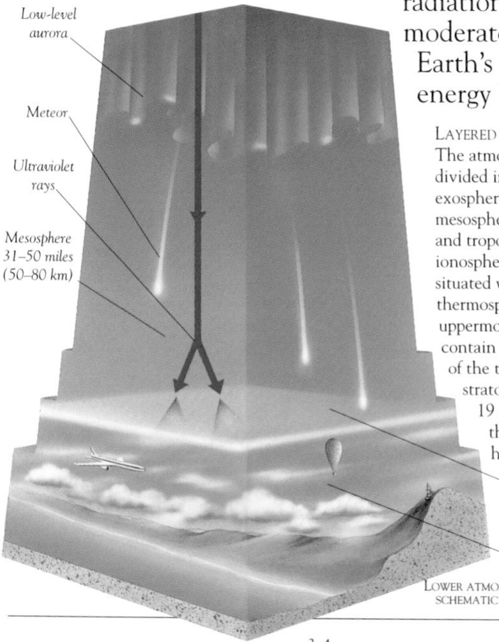

LAYERED STRUCTURE
The atmosphere is divided into five layers: exosphere, thermosphere, mesosphere, stratosphere, and troposphere. The ionosphere region is situated within the thermosphere. The three uppermost layers together contain only six percent of the total gases; the stratosphere has 19 percent, and the troposphere has 75 percent.

Low-level aurora

Meteor

Ultraviolet rays

Mesosphere
31–50 miles
(50–80 km)

Stratosphere
7–31 miles
(12–50 km)

Troposphere
0–7 miles
(0–12 km)

LOWER ATMOSPHERE:
SCHEMATIC VIEW

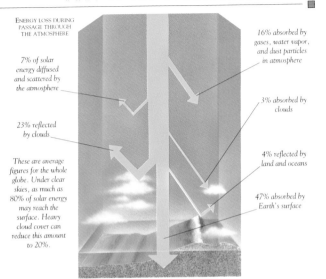

ENERGY LOSS DURING
PASSAGE THROUGH
THE ATMOSPHERE

7% of solar
energy diffused
and scattered by
the atmosphere

23% reflected
by clouds

These are average
figures for the whole
globe. Under clear
skies, as much as
80% of solar energy
may reach the
surface. Heavy
cloud cover can
reduce this amount
to 20%.

16% absorbed by
gases, water vapor,
and dust particles
in atmosphere

3% absorbed by
clouds

4% reflected by
land and oceans

47% absorbed by
Earth's surface

14 miles
(22 km)

12 miles
(19 km)

10 miles
(16 km)

8 miles
(13 km)

6 miles
(10 km)

ENERGY BUDGET
More than half the energy
in sunlight is lost through
absorption, reflection, and
scattering. The scattering of
light by gas molecules and
dust particles accounts for
the blue color of the sky.
The sky is lightest blue near
the surface, where there is
the most gas and dust.
With increasing height,
blue turns to black.

ATMOSPHERE FACTS

• The total mass of air
in the atmosphere is
about 5,600 trillion tons
(tonnes).

• The coldest part of
the atmosphere is about
53–60 miles (85–95 km)
above the surface where
temperatures are usually
about –130°F (–90°C).

WHERE THE WEATHER IS

MOST WEATHER is confined to the troposphere. This is the most active part of the atmosphere, and the air here is in constant motion. The troposphere contains almost all of the atmosphere's water vapor, which in places becomes visible as clouds.

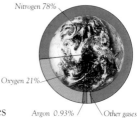

Nitrogen 78%

Oxygen 21%

Argon 0.93%

Other gases 0.07%

COMPOSITION OF DRY AIR
The troposphere also contains on average about 2–4 percent water.

The tops of storm clouds can reach heights of 9 miles (15 km)

Cirrus clouds form near the top of the troposphere

The boundary region between the troposphere and the stratosphere is called the tropopause

Most clouds form at heights below about 7 miles (12 km)

Mountains help shape the motion of the troposphere. They force air to flow around them or rise over them.

A SEA OF AIR
Air is a fluid in constant motion. This motion is the result of inequalities in temperature and pressure between different parts of the troposphere. The world's weather is the result of the troposphere's natural tendency to equalize temperature and pressure.

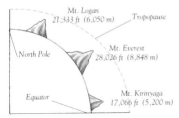

Mt. Logan
21,333 ft (6,050 m)

Tropopause

North Pole

Mt. Everest
28,026 ft (8,848 m)

Equator

Mt. Kirinyaga
17,066 ft (5,200 m)

TROPOPAUSE

The height of the tropopause varies with geographical latitude. At the poles, the average height is about 6 miles (9 km) above sea level. At the equator, the average height is about 10 miles (16 km). The tallest mountains reach about three-quarters of the way to the tropopause.

ATMOSPHERIC MOTION

The atmosphere moves because of warm and cold air. Warm air rises (A), and decreases in pressure. The rising air is replaced by air drawn in from the surrounding area. Cool air sinks (B), and increases in pressure. When cool air reaches the surface it spreads out.

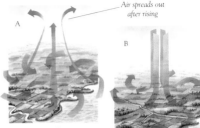

Air spreads out after rising

A

B

Air spreads out after descending

DATA: GASES IN THE ATMOSPHERE			
Constant	% volume	Variable	% volume
Nitrogen	78.08	Carbon dioxide	0.034
Oxygen	20.95	Carbon monoxide	0.01
Argon	0.93	Ozone	0.001
Neon	0.0018	Sulfur dioxide	0.0001
Helium	0.00052	Nitrogen dioxide	0.00002
Methane	0.00015	Water vapor	0–4.0*
Krypton	0.00011		
Hydrogen	0.0000.5	*When water vapor is present, the other constituents are reduced in proportion	
Xenon	0.000008		

ATMOSPHERE FACTS

• The total mass of water vapor in the atmosphere at any time is 146 trillion tons (tonnes).

• Ozone is a special form of oxygen gas. Ozone molecules have three oxygen atoms instead of two.

TEMPERATURE AND PRESSURE

WE THINK OF temperature in terms of whether it is a hot or cold day – the temperature close to the Earth's surface. We cannot feel air pressure in the same way, but it is equally important. The distribution of temperature and pressure throughout the atmosphere is crucial to the working of the weather machine.

A WARM DAY?
On the beach it is warm. Some 10,000 ft (3,000 m) overhead, however, the temperature is well below the freezing point.

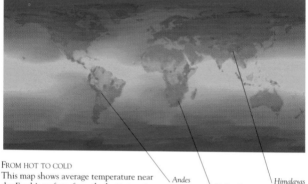

FROM HOT TO COLD
This map shows average temperature near the Earth's surface, from the hottest regions (yellow) to the coldest regions (deep blue). Mountain ranges show up as colder than the surrounding areas.

Andes

Drakensberg mountains

Himalayas

Cooler, lower
pressure air

Warmer, higher
pressure air

PRESSURE AND TEMPERATURE
Vertical differences in air temperature are
closely linked to air pressure. In general, air
pressure (often called atmospheric pressure)
is greatest at sea level, where the air is densest.
On a mountain peak, the air is less dense and
the pressure is lower. The air temperature is
usually lower than it would be at sea level.

*A pressure gradient exists
between high pressure at A and
low pressure at B*

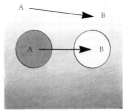

ATMOSPHERIC MOTION
Like other fluids, air tends toward a
state where all regions at the same
altitude have equal pressure. As a result,
air flows from regions of high pressure to
regions of low pressure. The difference
between two adjoining regions can be
described as a pressure gradient, and air
flows "down" the gradient.

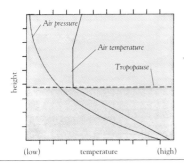

LAPSE RATE
Air pressure and air temperature
both decrease away from the
Earth's surface. The rate of
pressure decrease is constant, but
the temperature decrease is
variable and depends on the water
content (humidity) of the air. The
rate of decrease is known as the
lapse rate. The lapse rate for dry
air is about 5.5°F per 1,000 ft
(1.0°C per 100 m).

AIR MASSES

PROLONGED HIGH PRESSURE can cause parts of the atmosphere to become stagnant. The resulting air masses take on the weather characteristics of the region in which they formed. When these air masses start moving, they carry their weather with them, especially to the midlatitudes.

AIR MASS MARKERS
Cumulus clouds like these are typical of a maritime polar air mass.

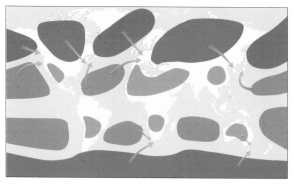

MAIN MASSES
This map shows the basic distribution of the different air masses that influence the weather. The size and locations of individual air masses are approximate because they change constantly.

MARITIME POLAR
CONTINENTAL POLAR
CONTINENTAL TROPICAL
MARITIME TROPICAL

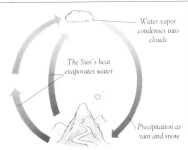

Water vapor condenses into clouds

The Sun's heat evaporates water

Precipitation as rain and snow

CLOSED CYCLE

Water circulates through the atmosphere as vapor, evaporating from land and oceans, and condensing to fall as precipitation. The amount of water vapor in a given air mass is called its humidity. Warm air can hold more water vapor than cold air. Air that cannot hold any more water vapor is said to be saturated.

ITCZ

The ITCZ (intertropical convergence zone) is marked by a narrow zone of cloud clusters that bring heavy rainfall. The ITCZ occurs because air streams from higher latitudes converge near the equator, forcing warm moist air to rise, cool, and condense into rain-bearing clouds.

DATA: AIR MASSES

Air Mass	Description
Maritime tropical (mT)	warm and very moist
Maritime polar (mP)	cool and fairly moist
Maritime arctic (mA)	cold and quite moist
Maritime antarctic (mAA)	very cold and fairly dry
Continental tropical (cT)	hot and dry
Continental polar (cP)	cold and dry
Continental arctic (cA)	very cold and dry
Continental antarctic (cAA)	very cold and dry

ATMOSPHERE FACTS

• Water has an average "residence period" in the atmosphere of 11 days before it falls as rain or snow.

• A tropical air mass contains about 5–10 times more water than a polar air mass of similar size.

OPTICAL EFFECTS

RAINBOW COLORS and other optical effects are the result of tiny particles in the air. During its passage through the atmosphere, sunlight is reflected, refracted, and scattered by water droplets, ice crystals, and atmospheric dust.

NATURAL SPECTRUM
A rainbow is the result of millions of raindrops acting like tiny prisms. They split sunlight into the colors of the spectrum and reflect them to the viewer's eye.

Refraction

Refraction

Reflection

The viewer sees just one color from each raindrop

Colors separate because different colors are refracted at different angles

Raindrop

Millions of reflections combine to produce the familiar spectrum

REFLECTED IMAGE
The colors of a rainbow are the colors of sunlight. The light is reflected from the inner surface of individual raindrops. As the sunlight enters and leaves a raindrop, it is refracted (bent). This refraction splits the light into its component colors: red, orange, yellow, green, blue, indigo, and violet.

THREE SUNS
Low in the sky above a frozen winter landscape, the Sun is bracketed by a halo and a pair of sun-dogs. The faint horizontal line through the three "suns" is a parhelic circle – another refraction effect which always appears parallel to the ground.

ICE LIGHT
A halo around the Sun is the result of light being reflected and refracted by ice crystals in thin, high-level clouds. In addition to circular halos, ice crystals can also produce various arcs (partial circles like rainbows) and parhelia (also called mock-suns or sun-dogs). Bright moonlight can also produce halos and paraselenae (mock-moons).

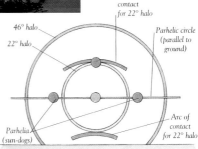

Arc of contact for 22° halo

46° halo

22° halo

Parhelic circle (parallel to ground)

Parhelia (sun-dogs)

Arc of contact for 22° halo

SUNBEAM
Rays of sunlight sometimes emerge from breaks in cloud like searchlight beams. The rays become visible when sunlight is scattered by dust or fine raindrops. The rays are in fact parallel, and the apparent spreading is a trick of perspective.

OPTICAL EFFECT FACT
• In late September 1950, a famous "blue moon" was visible across large parts of Europe and North America. The strange coloring was caused by smoke from massive forest fires in the Rocky Mountains.

SURFACE FACTORS

OCEANS AND SEAS

SEAWATER COVERS about 70 percent of the Earth's surface. Ocean currents are a major influence on climate and weather. Surface currents are produced by the winds, and follow the same general directions. The surface currents play a major role in transferring heat from the Tropics to the polar regions.

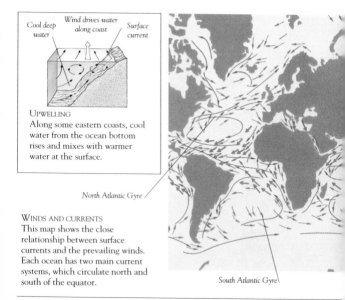

Cool deep water   *Wind drives water along coast*   *Surface current*

UPWELLING
Along some eastern coasts, cool water from the ocean bottom rises and mixes with warmer water at the surface.

North Atlantic Gyre

WINDS AND CURRENTS
This map shows the close relationship between surface currents and the prevailing winds. Each ocean has two main current systems, which circulate north and south of the equator.

South Atlantic Gyre

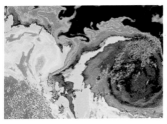

OCEAN GYRES
Large surface circulation systems are
known as gyres. This satellite image
shows a part of the North Atlantic gyre
formed by the Gulf Stream current off
the east coast of North America. The
mixing of cold water (black) from the
Labrador Current with much warmer
Gulf Stream water (yellow), produces a
gyre of warm water (green). There are
similar gyres in the other oceans.

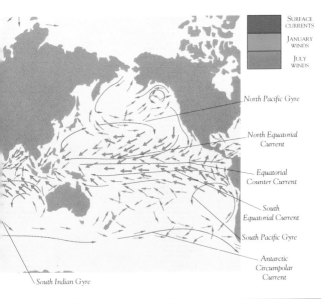

SURFACE
CURRENTS

JANUARY
WINDS

JULY
WINDS

North Pacific Gyre

North Equatorial
Current

Equatorial
Counter Current

South
Equatorial Current

South Pacific Gyre

Antarctic
Circumpolar
Current

South Indian Gyre

SEACOASTS

THE SEA WARMS UP and cools down more slowly than land. At certain times of year, temperature contrasts can occur between the sea and adjoining land areas. These contrasts produce a daily pattern of land and sea breezes. On a global scale, temperature contrasts are responsible for the effect known as continentality.

BREEZE BENT
Repeated exposure to a strong onshore breeze has forced this cliff-top tree to grow almost parallel to the ground.

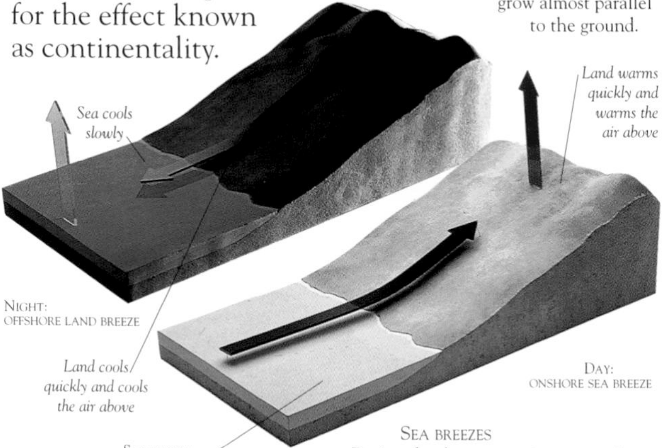

Land warms quickly and warms the air above

Sea cools slowly

NIGHT:
OFFSHORE LAND BREEZE

Land cools quickly and cools the air above

Sea warms slowly

DAY:
ONSHORE SEA BREEZE

SEA BREEZES
During the day, warm air can rise above the land. Cool air can flow across the coastline to replace it, creating a strong sea breeze. At night, cool air can sink over land, creating a weak land breeze.

AVERAGE SEA TEMPERATURES DURING FEBRUARY

77+°F (25+°C)
68–77°F (20–25°C)
59–68°F (15–20°C)
50–59°F (10–15°C)
41–50°F (5–10°C)
32–41°F (0–5°C)
32°F (0°C)

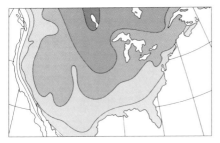

CONTINENTALITY

This map shows annual temperature variation (the darker the shading the greater the variation). Inland areas have a large variation – this effect is known as continentality. Near the coast, the moderating influence of the sea produces a much smaller variation.

DATA BOX: WARM AND COLD OCEAN CURRENTS		
Agulhas	warm	East African coast
Alaska	warm	North American coast
Benguela	cold	South African coast
Brazil	cold	South American coast
California	cold	North American coast
Guinea	warm	West African coast
Humboldt (Peru)	cold	South American coast
Kuroshio	warm	Sea of Japan
Labrador	cold	North American coast
Oyashio	cold	Siberian coast

SEACOAST FACTS

• At 91°F (33°C) the warmest sea-surface water in the world is found in the Gulf between Qatar and Bahrain island.

• A sea breeze can lower temperatures on land by 21°F (12°C).

EL NIÑO

AN IRREGULAR Pacific Ocean
current affects the weather across
25 percent of the Earth's surface.
This current, called El Niño,
forms part of a larger system
called the Southern Oscillation.
When El Niño occurs, the result
can be droughts and floods in
areas as far apart as Australia and
the United States.

TIME OF DROUGHT
The 1982–83 El Niño
caused serious drought in
Australia. Dry conditions
produced bushfires that
killed 65 people.

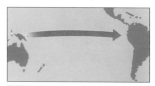

REVERSE FLOW
In normal years, cool, deep water rises
to the surface off the South American
coast and is warmed. A warm current
flows westward from South America.

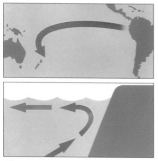

WARM OVER COLD
The El Niño current flows eastward,
bringing warmer water to the South
American coast, and stopping the cool,
deep water from reaching the surface.

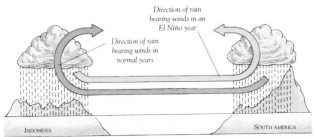

Direction of rain
bearing winds in an
El Niño year

Direction of rain
bearing winds in
normal years

INDONESIA

SOUTH AMERICA

INDONESIAN RAINFALL

In normal years (red), warm moist air is
carried westward from South America.
The moisture is released over Indonesia
as heavy rain.

INDONESIAN DROUGHT

When an El Niño occurs (yellow), wind
direction is reversed, bringing heavy
rains to the South American coast and
leaving Indonesia in drought.

Rare hurricane
hits Hawaii

Drought kills crops in
India and Sri Lanka

Flooding and
mudslides in
coastal states

GLOBAL REACH

The 1982–83 El Niño disrupted weather patterns
around the world. Unusually high water temperatures
killed coral reefs across the Pacific, and caused the
collapse of the South American fishing industry.

EL NIÑO FACTS

• The current is called
El Niño (which means
"boy child") because it
tends to appear around
Christmastime.

• An El Niño event
in 1976–77 produced
months of drought
followed by the worst
winter on record for
the United States.

• On average an
El Niño occurs about
14 times per century.

BARRIERS

MOUNTAINS CREATE their own climate, and their influence on the weather extends far and wide. Mountain ranges form barriers to the free flow of air in the lower atmosphere. Air is forced to rise up over them. This enforced lifting cools the air and can create wave motion in the atmosphere.

SHAPED FLOW
Air flowing up the slope of the land has shaped the clouds at the edge of this mountain precipice.

Over the sea, air flows parallel to the surface

Air rises slightly over a low hill

Mountain creates wave in atmosphere

Air forced to rise over mountains

CONTROLLING EFFECT
In midlatitudes, the prevailing winds near the Earth's surface blow from west to east. Mountain ranges that run north–south, such as the Rockies or the Andes, block the smooth flow of air, and help shape the weather. These mountains prevent moist Pacific Ocean air from reaching the interiors of the American continents. The Himalayas and the Alps are also important in shaping weather.

WAVE FORMATION BY HILLS AND MOUNTAINS

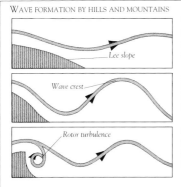

Lee slope

The shape of the lee slope affects the shape of the waves. A shallow gradient produces a fairly shallow wave.

Wave crest

Air descending a steeper slope produces more pronounced waves. The crest of the wave is closer to the lee slope.

Rotor turbulence

Air flowing down a cliff face produces steep waves, and may also produce rotor turbulence near the base of the cliff.

Air follows slope of land

SNOWCAP

Air cools as it rises, and if it rises to a sufficient height, it cools below freezing point. Any moisture left in the air is liable to fall as snow, giving the mountain a white cap.

SNOWLINE

The height at which snow remains on mountains throughout the year – the snowline – depends on latitude. The nearer the pole, the lower the snowline. The tree line marks the upper limit of tree growth.

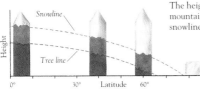

Snowline

Tree line

Height

0°   30°   Latitude   60°   90°

ABSORBING HEAT

AIR TEMPERATURES near the
Earth's surface depend on the
temperature of the land beneath.
Different soils and plants absorb
differing amounts of solar energy.
Cities and lakes also influence
the air above them.

COOL FOREST
Green forests absorb large
amounts of heat, but they
remain cool because much
of the energy is used in
evapotranspiration.

HEAT TRANSFER
Air is heated or cooled by contact with the
Earth's surface. The model below shows how
different surfaces can cause air to rise or fall.

*Air tends to
descend over
cool forests*

*Cities create their
own heat and
produce rising air*

*Air often
sinks over seas
and lakes*

*Plowed fields absorb heat
and cause air to rise*

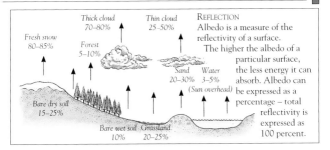

REFLECTION

Albedo is a measure of the reflectivity of a surface. The higher the albedo of a particular surface, the less energy it can absorb. Albedo can be expressed as a percentage – total reflectivity is expressed as 100 percent.

Thick cloud 70–80%
Thin cloud 25–50%
Fresh snow 80–85%
Forest 5–10%
Sand 20–30%
Water 3–5% (*Sun overhead*)
Bare dry soil 15–25%
Bare wet soil 10%
Grassland 20–25%

HEAT ISLAND

Cities are very complex surface features. Construction materials, such as concrete and asphalt, absorb heat on sunny days and release it slowly at night. As a result, cities are usually a few degrees warmer at night than surrounding areas, especially when there is little or no wind to mix the atmosphere.

LAKES

Inland bodies of water can create their own circulation systems. A lake heats up more slowly than the surrounding land, causing the air above it to sink. The descending air creates a lake breeze. Cold air from Canada flowing over the warmer Great Lakes creates a "lake effect." Moisture evaporating off the lakes falls as snow in the US.

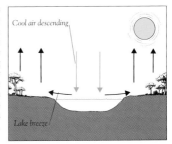

Cool air descending

Lake breeze

VOLCANOES

ERUPTING VOLCANOES hurl hot ash and scalding gases into the air. But their main effect on climate and weather is to make conditions cooler. The heat of the eruption is quickly dissipated. Volcanic dust-particles and gases, however, can remain in the atmosphere for two years or more, reducing sunlight and lowering temperatures.

MOUNT ST. HELENS
In the 1980 eruption, the blast was directed sideways and comparatively little volcanic material entered the upper atmosphere.

VOLCANIC DUST, ASH, AND GAS
Small particles of dust and ash reach the stratosphere, where they spread out to form a thin, sun-absorbing cloud. Sulfur dioxide gas combines with water vapor to form microscopic droplets of sulfuric acid, which absorb even more sunlight than dust. Emissions from the Tambora eruption lowered temperatures world-wide by about 1.2°F (0.7°C) in 1815, which became widely known as the "year without a summer."

40 billion tons (tonnes)

9 billion tons (tonnes)

500 million tons (tonnes)

500 million tons (tonnes)

Figures give total amount of ejecta (dust, ash, and gas)

TAMBORA, INDONESIA 1815

KRAKATAU, INDONESIA 1883

ST. HELENS, US 1980

EL CHICHON, MEXICO 1982

April 5: plume
shows up on
satellite images

April 15: plume
reaches Asia

April 25: plume
stretches around
the world

SPEED OF SPREAD
When volcanic particles enter the upper atmosphere, they are
blown into a long plume by high-level winds. These maps are
based on satellite images, and show the rapid spread of the plume
from El Chichon, which erupted in Mexico on April 3, 1982.

Volcanic plume

EL CHICHON
The El Chichon volcano erupted in
a remote and sparsely inhabited part
of Mexico. As a result, scientists
only learned about the eruption
when it showed up on satellite
images (see above). This photograph
shows the crater left by the eruption.

SUNSET SPECTACULAR
Volcanic eruptions often
cause spectacular optical
effects for a long time
afterward. This dramatic
sunset was colored by
El Chichon ash and dust
more than eight months
after the eruption.

VOLCANO FACT
• Recent research has
shown that the droplets
of sulfuric acid,
produced as a result of
volcanic eruptions,
have a much greater
sunlight-blocking (and
therefore temperature-
reducing) effect than
either dust or ash.

TEMPERATURE

SUNLIGHT

TEMPERATURES ON EARTH depend
on energy from the Sun. This
energy is not distributed evenly
across Earth's surface. On a global
scale, the distribution depends
on the angle at which sunlight
reaches the ground. Clouds may
also absorb heat energy before
it reaches the ground.

SOAKING UP THE SUN
In California's Death Valley,
the temperature frequently
rises above 122°F (50°C).

*Near a pole, about 5% of solar heat
energy reaches the surface*

*In the midlatitudes, about
50-60% reaches the surface*

*At the equator, about 75% of solar
heat energy reaches the surface*

ENERGY DISTRIBUTION
The energy delivered by sunlight
varies with latitude. Away from the
equator, the Earth's curved surface
means that each "beam" of sunlight is
spread over a greater area, and must pass
through a greater thickness of atmosphere.

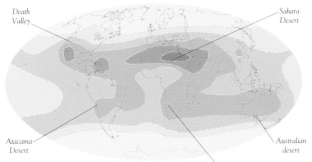

Death Valley

Sahara Desert

Atacama Desert

Australian desert

Kalahari Desert

WHERE THE SUNSHINE IS
This map shows the annual average amount of solar energy reaching a horizontal surface at ground level. The greatest amounts (darkest shading) occur in the midlatitude deserts where the atmosphere is usually clear and cloud-free. The smallest amounts (lightest shading) occur in polar regions, which are shrouded in cloud and fog for much of the year. Clouds near the equator also reduce the amount of sunlight.

DATA BOX: HEAT STRESS INDEX		
Caution	80°–90°F (27°–32°C)	Fatigue possible with prolonged exposure and activity.
Extreme caution	90°–105°F (32°–41°C)	Sunstroke and cramps possible with prolonged activity.
Danger	105°–130°F (41°–55°C)	Sunstroke, cramps, and heat exhaustion likely, heatstroke possible.
Extreme danger	above 130°F (above 55°C)	Heatstroke or sunstroke imminent.

COLD AND SUNLESS
Antarctica, which spends up to half the year in darkness, is the coldest place on Earth. At Vostok, a minimum temperature of –132°F (–91°C) was recorded in 1983.

DAY AND NIGHT

EARTH'S ROTATION produces
a pattern of light and darkness
that changes with latitude. Near
the equator, day and night are of
almost equal length throughout
the year. In the midlatitudes,
the pattern is one of long winter
nights and short summer nights.
At high latitudes (near the poles)
day and night each last for almost
six months in the "lands of the
midnight sun."

DIVIDING LINE
The terminator, the line
that marks the difference
between day and night,
moves along the equator at
a speed of about 1,000 mph
(1,600 km/h).

SIX-MONTH DAY
The tilt of Earth's axis
means that polar regions
have six months of
winter, followed by six
months of summer. In
the middle of the polar
summer, the Sun does
not set, but remains
above the horizon for 24
hours per day (as shown
at right). Similarly, in
midwinter there is
complete darkness
– the Sun stays below
the horizon all day.

MIDNIGHT SUN AS SEEN FROM
THE NORTH COAST OF
SCANDINAVIA IN MID-JULY

The photograph at the
beginning of the sequence was
taken at 7pm on July 21. The
photograph at far right was
taken at 5pm on July 22.

At midnight, the Sun is
at its lowest point in the
sky, but has not set

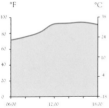

°F   °C

DESERT CONTRASTS
Day/night temperature contrasts are most evident in midlatitude deserts. These graphs show the air temperature changes over 24 hours in the Sahara Desert during summer.

NIGHT AND DAY
Sunlight is strongest at midday, but its warming effect is cumulative. The warmest time of the day is usually in the afternoon. The coldest time is often just before dawn.

°F   °C

TEMPERATURE FACTS
• The most consistently hot days occur at Dallol on the fringe of the Danakil Depression in Ethiopia. Daytime temperatures exceed 100°F (38°C) on an average of 295 days per year.

• The greatest change over 24 hr occurred at Browning, Montana, on January 16, 1916 when temperatures fell by 100°F (55°C).

As the day goes on, the Sun rises higher in the sky

At midday, the Sun is at its highest point in the sky

HOT AND COLD AIR

WARM AIR RISES, cool air sinks, and warm air holds more moisture than cold air. These are the fundamental principles behind the workings of the weather. Where warm air is rising, the atmosphere is said to be unstable. Where cool air is sinking (known as subsidence), the atmosphere is described as stable.

THREE PHASES
On Earth, H$_2$O (water) exists in three states – as a solid, a liquid, and a gas. Changes between these states are involved in most weather processes.

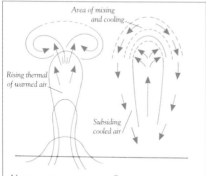

Area of mixing and cooling

Rising thermal of warmed air

Subsiding cooled air

UNSTABLE AIR
Air near the ground is warmed and forms a rising convection current of air known as a thermal.

STABLE AIR
When a thermal cools to the same temperature as its surroundings, the air starts to subside.

TEMPERATURE FACTS
• Evaporation removes large amounts of heat from Earth's surface. The amount of heat energy required to vaporize a quantity of liquid water at 212°F (100°C) is more than five times the amount of heat energy that is required to raise the temperature of the same quantity of water from 32°F (0°C) to 212°F (100°C).

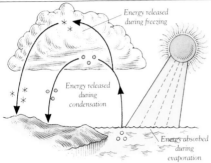

Energy released
during freezing

Energy released
during
condensation

Energy absorbed
during
evaporation

ENERGY TRANSFER
Changes in state circulate
energy between Earth and
atmosphere. The Sun
provides energy to
evaporate water. When
water vapor condenses in
clouds, energy is released.
Still more energy is
released if the condensed
water droplets then freeze
into ice particles.

INVERTED STATE
A temperature inversion
occurs when the normal
decrease in temperature
with height is reversed
(inverted). This can
happen when a layer of
warm air is trapped by a
subsiding layer of cooler air.
Inversions are often
associated with clear skies.

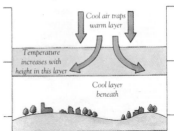

Cool air traps
warm layer

Temperature
increases with
height in this layer

Cool layer
beneath

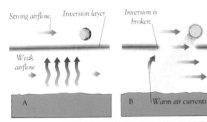

Strong airflow   Inversion layer

Weak
airflow

A

Inversion is
broken

B   Warm air currents

BELOW THE FLOW
Inversions often form
beneath an upper-level
airflow (A). The
inversion is dissolved
(B) when heat from
the Sun creates rising
air currents which
break through the
inversion layer.

DEW AND FROST

EVEN THE DRIEST AIR contains some water vapor. If the air is cooled sufficiently, at night for instance, some of the water vapor will condense on surfaces as dew. The temperature at which air can no longer hold all the water it contains is called its dew point. Further cooling may lower the temperature to freezing point and produce a white frost.

MORNING DEW
These grasses provide an ideal surface for the condensation of dew. As the day warms up, the dew will evaporate into the air.

Clouds reradiate heat back to Earth

Heat radiation is lost to space

CLOUD COVER
At night, the Earth loses heat by radiation. Clouds block this heat loss and reradiate some heat back to Earth. Temperatures usually remain above the dew point.

NO CLOUD COVER
The Earth loses heat rapidly, and cools the layer of air just above the ground. Temperatures can fall to the dew point and water (dew) condenses on surfaces.

CRYSTAL COATING
Frost occurs when the air
temperature near the
ground falls below freezing
point. Water vapor freezes
into ice crystals, which are
deposited on vegetation
and other exposed surfaces.
Frost is a major hazard to
farmers across the world.
Temperatures below 32°F
(0°C) can damage, and
even kill, plants.

FROST POCKETS
Cool air sinks, and on
windless nights cold
air will flow gently down
hillsides. The cool air
tends to accumulate in the
valley bottoms, where it
causes frequent frosts.
Frost-prone locations are
popularly known as "frost-
hollows" or "frost-pockets."

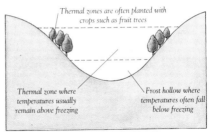

*Thermal zones are often planted with
crops such as fruit trees*

*Thermal zone where
temperatures usually
remain above freezing*

*Frost hollow where
temperatures often fall
below freezing*

TYPES OF FROST
A white frost is often
called a ground frost, but
is more correctly termed a
hoarfrost. Other frost
effects include rime, which
forms in cold foggy
conditions. Rime often
looks like hoarfrost, but
the deposits are thicker.

DEW FACT
• At Abu Dhabi on
the eastern coast of the
Arabian peninsula, the
annual rainfall is 4 in
(10 cm). Dew deposits
add the equivalent of
another 2 in (5 cm) to
the total precipitation.

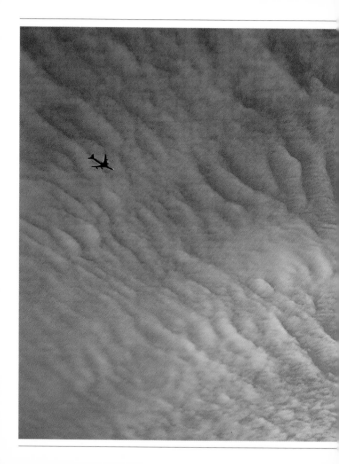

CLOUD

FORMATION

CLOUDS FORM when rising air cools to a point where it can no longer hold any more water vapor. The vapor condenses in the form of tiny water droplets. Clouds often form when air rises over warm ground, or when air is forced to rise over high ground. Cloud formations are classified according to their shape and height, and the main formations have been given Latin names.

FAIR WEATHER CUMULUS
Small white cumulus clouds like these (elongated and narrow) are a fairly reliable sign of good weather.

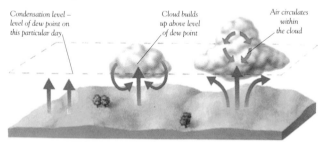

Condensation level – level of dew point on this particular day

Cloud builds up above level of dew point

Air circulates within the cloud

THERMAL START
Air is heated by contact with sun-warmed ground. The warm air rises in a series of thermals.

CONDENSATION
Rising air cools. Above the level of the dew point, a cloud forms as water droplets condense.

CIRCULATION
Warm air continues to rise, providing additional water vapor for the cloud's growth.

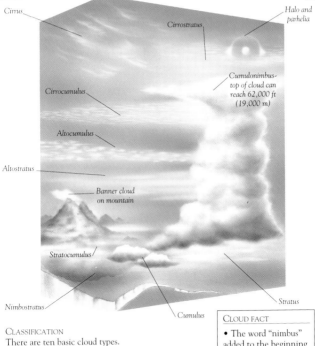

Cirrus

Cirrostratus

Halo and parhelia

Cumulonimbus-top of cloud can reach 62,000 ft (19,000 m)

Cirrocumulus

Altocumulus

Altostratus

Banner cloud on mountain

Stratocumulus

Nimbostratus

Cumulus

Stratus

CLASSIFICATION
There are ten basic cloud types.
Cirrus, cirrocumulus, and cirrostratus are high-level clouds, typically 3–7 miles (5–11 km) above sea level. Altostratus and altocumulus are medium-level clouds, typically 1.5–3 miles (3–5 km) above the ground. Stratus, stratocumulus, cumulus, cumulonimbus, and nimbostratus are low-level clouds – their cloud-base (the bottom of the clouds) is below 1.5 miles (3 km).

CLOUD FACT
• The word "nimbus" added to the beginning or end of a cloud type, e.g., cumulonimbus or nimbostratus, means that the cloud is a rain cloud, and will usually appear to be dark gray.

SPECIAL SHAPES

CLOUD SHAPES are influenced both by winds and by the shape of the Earth beneath. Steady (laminar) winds and irregular (turbulent) winds produce different cloud shapes. Mountains often create their own special clouds. Wave motion in the atmosphere can also produce interesting visual effects.

LENTICULAR CLOUDS
Looking like invading alien spaceships, these lenticular (lens-shaped) clouds were photographed downwind of the Cascade mountains in California.

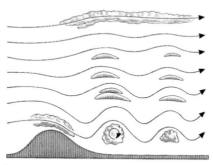

LEE-WAVE CLOUDS
Mountains often create standing waves in the atmosphere on the lee (downwind) side. Lenticular clouds may form at the top of each wave. These remain stationary, because they are "fixed" to the waves. Rotor clouds are sometimes formed by turbulence near the surface.

CLOUD FACTS
• Clouds formed as a result of air rising over mountains are known as orographic clouds.

• Aircraft produce contrails (condensation trails) when flying through air colder than freezing point. Water emitted by the engines freezes into ice cystals.

• Cumulus clouds sometimes form over power stations, and are called "fumulus" clouds.

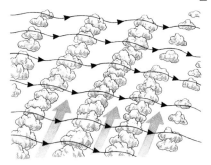

CROSSING STREETS
These peculiar linear cloud patterns are the result of jet-aircraft contrails slicing through cloud streets.

CLOUD STREETS (above)
Gentle winds often produce lines of cumulus clouds arranged in cloud streets. The windflow above may be deflected into waves.

STORMY BILLOWS (left)
Mamma (or mammatocumulus) clouds are rounded structures that are sometimes seen on the lower surface of certain clouds, especially cumulonimbus (storm clouds).

VISIBLE WAVES
Occasionally, clouds reveal wave motion in the atmosphere very clearly indeed. These perfectly formed "breakers" in mountain stratus clouds indicate the presence of Kelvin-Helmholtz (K-H) waves. These waves are caused by differing wind speeds in two adjacent levels of the atmosphere.

FOG, MIST, AND HAZE

REDUCED VISIBILITY near the ground is caused by tiny particles suspended in the air. Water droplets that cause a moderate reduction in visibility are called mist. Those causing a serious visibility problem are called fog. Mists and fogs often form over seas, rivers, and lakes. Particles of dust, smoke, or salt that affect the clarity of the air are collectively known as haze.

FOG BANKS
Advection fog is common in the northwest Atlantic. Thick fogs often form over cold, shallow, offshore waters, such as the Grand Banks off Newfoundland.

Warm air traps fog near sea surface

Wind direction

High land prevents fog from moving very far inland

ADVECTION FOG
When warm, moist air blows over a cold sea (or lake), it produces an advection fog. Moisture in the warm airstream is cooled by contact with the cold water surface and condenses into droplets. The warm air keeps the fog trapped near the surface.

FOG WATERED

The only moisture that reaches the coastal Namib Desert of southwestern Africa comes in the form of sea fog. The fog forms when warm, moist air is blown over the cold waters of the offshore Benguela current. The air is cooled and fog droplets condense.

VALLEY FOG

Morning fog fills a valley in Yellowstone National Park, Wyoming. Away from coasts, fog often forms on calm, clear nights (known as "radiation nights"). The land radiates heat into space and the air rapidly cools to the dew point. Radiation fog tends to collect in valleys and other "frost hollows."

STEAM FOG

When very cold, dry air flows over warm water, the lowest level of air absorbs water vapor, which then condenses as whispy steam fog, also known as Arctic Sea Smoke.

FOG FACTS

• Fog – visibility below 1,100 yards (1,000 m) – mainly affects aircraft.

• Thick fog – visibility 55–220 yards (50–200 m) – dangerous for road traffic.

• Dense fog – visibility below 55 yards (50 m) – seriously disrupts all forms of transportation.

PRECIPITATION

WATER CYCLE

PRECIPITATION IS THE downward part of the water cycle. Rainfall is the major form in much of the world, others include snow, hail, dew, frost, and fog. The water cycle operates because air absorbs and releases water like a sponge.

THE WATER CYCLE

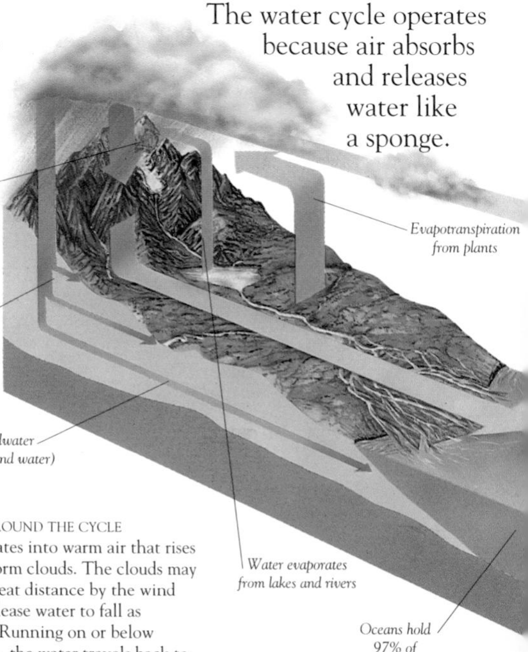

Precipitation as rain and/or snow on high ground

Evapotranspiration from plants

Water seeps into rocks

Groundwater (underground water)

Water evaporates from lakes and rivers

Oceans hold 97% of Earth's water

TRAVELING AROUND THE CYCLE

Water evaporates into warm air that rises and cools to form clouds. The clouds may be carried a great distance by the wind before they release water to fall as precipitation. Running on or below Earth's surface, the water travels back to the sea. The cycle repeats itself endlessly.

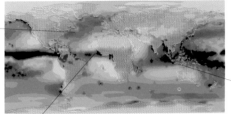

Rainfall associated with Gulf Stream

Worldwide band of rainfall associated with the ITCZ

Mainly seasonal monsoon rainfall

DISTRIBUTION OF ANNUAL RAINFALL
This map shows the total rainfall on the Earth's surface, including the 77 percent of the total that falls on the oceans. All the wettest places (darkest shading) are located near the intertropical convergence zone.

Clouds form as water vapor condenses

Rain falls over oceans

Water evaporates from ocean surface

PRECIPITATION FACTS

• Water that has fallen from the sky is known scientifically as "meteoric" water.

• The amount of water held in the atmosphere at any time is sufficient to produce about 1 in (2.5 cm) of rain over the surface of the Earth.

• The total amount of precipitation in one year is 5,000 trillion tons (tonnes).

• The average raindrop has a million times more water than the average cloud droplet.

WHY IT RAINS

RAINCLOUDS CAN FORM through one of three main processes. Orographic rainclouds form over hills and mountains. Convective rainclouds form in hot, humid conditions. Frontal rainclouds form when two air masses meet.

Orographic "feeder" clouds are "seeded" by raindrops from high-level clouds

Heaviest rainfall on upper windward slopes

Cool air

OROGRAPHIC
RAINFALL
Moist air cools and forms clouds as it rises over mountains. Rain falls on the windward slopes, while the leeward side remains dry.

Warm air

Moist air is blown up the windward side

CONVECTIVE RAINCLOUDS:
FORMATION, GROWTH, AND DISPERSION

CLOUDS FORM
The Sun evaporates water and creates rising thermals. Moist air cools and forms small clouds.

CLOUDS MULTIPLY
Continued heating by the Sun creates more thermals and produces more clouds.

CLOUDS AMALGAMATE
Small clouds clump together to form a larger cloud, which increases in size and height.

SEEDER-FEEDER RAINFALL
Fine raindrops fall from high-level frontal "seeder" clouds over mountains. As the raindrops pass through an orographic "feeder" cloud, they increase in size producing heavy rainfall on windward slopes.

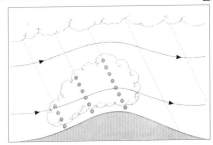

The leeward slope is in the rain shadow of the mountains and remains dry

IN THE SHADOW
Patagonia, in Argentina, lies in the rain shadow of the Andes. Moist air from the Pacific is cooled as it lifts over the mountains, and releases its moisture as rain. The air that reaches Patagonia is too dry to produce much rain and has created a rain-shadow desert.

Turret

MATURE CLOUD
A mature cloud contains strong internal upcurrents and may develop a number of "turrets."

Anvil

RAINFALL
The cloud-top spreads out in an anvil. Rain falls from the lower cloud producing downdrafts.

BREAK UP
The downdrafts become more powerful than the upcurrent, and the cloud starts to break up.

RAINDROPS

WATER CANNOT CONDENSE in pure air – the process requires a "condensation nucleus." Most of the condensation nuclei that cause clouds and rain are naturally occurring particles of dust, salt, or smoke. But artificially created particles also have an effect.

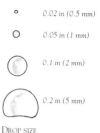

Illustrations magnified x2

° 0.02 in (0.5 mm)

○ 0.05 in (1 mm)

0.1 in (2 mm)

0.2 in (5 mm)

DROP SIZE
Drops range from less than 0.02 in (0.5 mm) to 0.2 in (5 mm). Drops larger than this break up on their way to the ground.

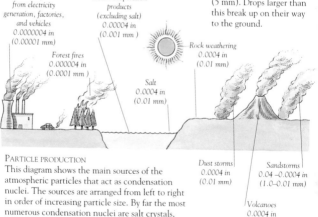

Combustion products
from electricity
generation, factories,
and vehicles
0.0000004 in
(0.00001 mm)

Forest fires
0.000004 in
(0.0001 mm)

Ocean evaporation
products
(excluding salt)
0.00004 in
(0.001 mm)

Salt
0.0004 in
(0.01 mm)

Rock weathering
0.0004 in
(0.01 mm)

Dust storms
0.0004 in
(0.01 mm)

Sandstorms
0.04 –0.0004 in
(1.0–0.01 mm)

Volcanoes
0.0004 in
(0.01 mm)

PARTICLE PRODUCTION
This diagram shows the main sources of the atmospheric particles that act as condensation nuclei. The sources are arranged from left to right in order of increasing particle size. By far the most numerous condensation nuclei are salt crystals, formed during the evaporation of seawater.

VOLCANIC ASH PARTICLE
0.0003 IN (0.008 MM) ACROSS

ALUMINA PARTICLE FROM JET
ENGINE EXHAUST
0.0005 IN (0.012 MM) ACROSS

ATMOSPHERIC DUST
Particles like these have been collected from near the tropopause by high-flying research aircraft. The photographs were taken with an electron microscope.

TROPICAL RAIN

In the warmer regions of the world, the level of the freezing point is above that of most clouds. Raindrops form inside clouds by coalescence. Small raindrops collide and join together, forming bigger drops that are heavy enough to fall to the surface.

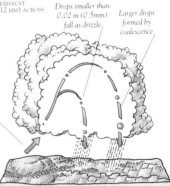

Drops smaller than 0.02 in (0.5mm) fall as drizzle

Larger drops formed by coalescence

Rising air

Water droplets freeze into ice crystals

Snowflakes melt, either inside cloud or on their way to the ground

Ice crystals grow into snowflakes and fall as snow

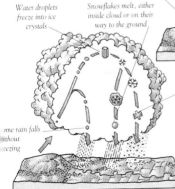

me rain falls ithout eezing

MELTED SNOW

In most parts of the world, most of the rain that falls to Earth is in fact melted snow. Tiny water droplets freeze into ice particles near the top of the cloud. The ice particles then grow into snowflakes, and melt to form raindrops.

SNOW

SNOW IS NOT frozen rain.
Snowflakes are created inside
clouds by tiny ice crystals
colliding and sticking together.
Most snowflakes melt on their
way to the ground and fall as
rain. Only when the air near the
ground is cold
enough will
snowflakes
fall as snow.

GRAPHIC SYMBOL	CRYSTAL SHAPE	TYPE
		Plate
		Stellar
		Column
		Needle
		Spatial dendrite
		Capped column
		Irregular

Small crystals of "dry" snow

In very cold, dry conditions, "diamond dust" ice crystals may fall

Plate crystal

Hexagonal (six-sided) snow crystal

SIX-SIDED WONDER
No two snow crystals have ever been found to be
identical. Details of their intricate structure can be
seen through a microscope. When it is very cold,
"dry" snow falls – the ice crystals do not stick together
easily, and the snow is fine and powdery. At
temperatures near freezing point, "wet" snow falls, and
large snowflakes form, especially if there is no wind.

DATA BOX: INUIT WORDS FOR SNOW

aniuk	snow used for drinking water
aqilluqqaaq	new, soft snow
ijaruvak	melting snow with ice crystals
isiriartaq	snow discolored by pollution
katakartanaq	snow with thin, hard crust
kinirtaq	damp, compact snow
masak	wet, saturated snow
maujaq	deep, soft snow
munnguqtuq	packed snow beginning to soften
niummak	hard snow on sea-ice
piqsiq	blowing snow (a blizzard)
pukak	dry, granular snow
qannialaaq	light, falling snow
qiqiqralijarnatuq	snow that is squeaky underfoot

SNOW FACTS

• Large stellar (star-shaped) snowflakes may grow to be 2–3 in (5–7 cm) across.

• The average snowfall for the North American continent is 40 in (102 cm) per year.

• During the 1971–72 winter, 975 in (2,477 cm) of snow fell at Mount Rainier, Washington.

SNOW COVER

Thick snow blankets the landscape in Yukon Territory, Canada. Snow lying on the ground is called snowpack, and is a useful and natural method of storing freshwater. In spring, when the snow starts to melt, the water will be released. Some will soak into the ground, while the rest will flow into streams and rivers.

SNOWROLLER

Sometimes, when fresh snow is moist enough to stick together, snowrollers may form on hillsides or in large fields. A snowroller is cylindrical in shape, and is blown by winds of more than 20 mph (12.5 km/h) until it grows too large to travel any farther. Snowrollers can reach nearly 4 ft (1.5 m) in diameter.

WIND

WIND SYSTEMS

WIND IS SIMPLY air in motion, moving from high pressure to low pressure. Winds are described by the direction they blow from – an easterly wind blows from the east, a westerly from the west. Prevailing winds (those that blow fairly steadily) are arranged in a series of belts around the globe. This pattern is the result of differences between the poles and the equator in rotational speed and solar heating.

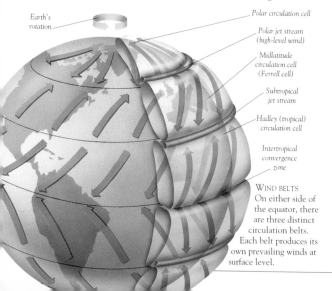

Earth's rotation

Polar circulation cell

Polar jet stream (high-level wind)

Midlatitude circulation cell (Ferrell cell)

Subtropical jet stream

Hadley (tropical) circulation cell

Intertropical convergence zone

WIND BELTS
On either side of the equator, there are three distinct circulation belts. Each belt produces its own prevailing winds at surface level.

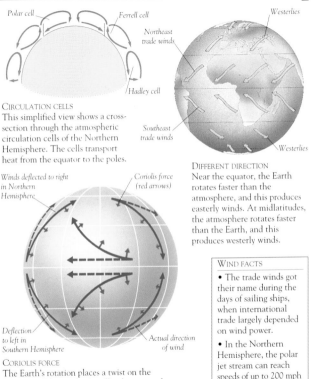

CIRCULATION CELLS
This simplified view shows a cross-section through the atmospheric circulation cells of the Northern Hemisphere. The cells transport heat from the equator to the poles.

Polar cell
Ferrell cell
Hadley cell

Westerlies
Northeast trade winds
Southeast trade winds
Westerlies

DIFFERENT DIRECTION
Near the equator, the Earth rotates faster than the atmosphere, and this produces easterly winds. At midlatitudes, the atmosphere rotates faster than the Earth, and this produces westerly winds.

Winds deflected to right in Northern Hemisphere
Coriolis force (red arrows)
Deflection to left in Southern Hemisphere
Actual direction of wind

CORIOLIS FORCE
The Earth's rotation places a twist on the direction of the winds. An effect known as the Coriolis force diverts the wind into a curved path. The Coriolis force is also responsible for the spiral winds in tornadoes and whirlwinds.

WIND FACTS
• The trade winds got their name during the days of sailing ships, when international trade largely depended on wind power.

• In the Northern Hemisphere, the polar jet stream can reach speeds of up to 200 mph (320 km/h), although 40–80 mph (65–130 km/h) is more usual.

COLD AND WARM FRONTS

THE POLAR JET STREAM marks the high-level boundary between polar and tropical air masses. Near or at the Earth's surface, the boundaries between air masses form a series of fronts. The stronger the contrast between the air masses, the more active the front, and the more weather it produces.

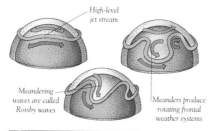

High-level jet stream

Meandering waves are called Rossby waves

Meanders produce rotating frontal weather systems

JET STREAM MEANDERS
The polar jet stream meanders gently from north to south as it encircles the globe. Beneath the jet stream, large frontal weather systems, such as depressions or "lows," form along the boundary between polar and tropical air masses.

FORMATION OF A FRONTAL WEATHER SYSTEM (MIDLATITUDE DEPRESSION)

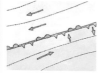

BOUNDARY FLOW
Initially, the boundary between polar and tropical air masses is smooth and the front is fairly straight.

SPINNING LOW
The air masses start to rotate around a low-pressure center, and separate warm and cold fronts develop.

ON THE MOVE
The bulge in the fronts has now developed into a characteristic kink. The mature weather system moves eastward.

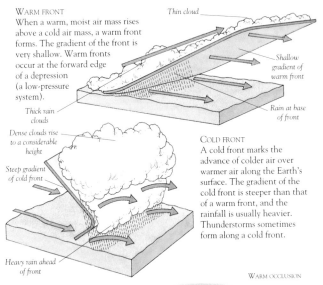

WARM FRONT
When a warm, moist air mass rises above a cold air mass, a warm front forms. The gradient of the front is very shallow. Warm fronts occur at the forward edge of a depression (a low-pressure system).

Thin cloud

Shallow gradient of warm front

Thick rain clouds

Rain at base of front

Dense clouds rise to a considerable height

Steep gradient of cold front

COLD FRONT
A cold front marks the advance of colder air over warmer air along the Earth's surface. The gradient of the cold front is steeper than that of a warm front, and the rainfall is usually heavier. Thunderstorms sometimes form along a cold front.

Heavy rain ahead of front

OCCLUSIONS
Depressions and other frontal systems are three-dimensional. Most depressions end when the cold front catches up with the warm front and cuts it off from the Earth's surface. If the cold front rises over the warm front, this is called a warm occlusion. If the cold front undercuts the warm front, this is called a cold occlusion.

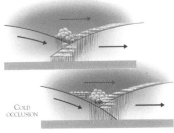

WARM OCCLUSION

COLD OCCLUSION

HIGHS AND LOWS

WEATHER IN THE midlatitudes is controlled by a sequence of high-pressure and low-pressure frontal weather systems. High-pressure systems, called anticyclones or "highs," usually bring fair weather. Low-pressure systems, called depressions or "lows," usually bring rain, or other precipitation, and very changeable conditions.

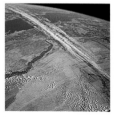

JET-STREAM CLOUDS
These clouds have been blown into elongated shapes by the jet stream.

FAMILY OF DEPRESSIONS
This illustration shows a family of three depressions at different stages of development. The upper picture shows the shape of the depressions viewed from above. The lower picture shows the systems in cross-section along the line A–B.

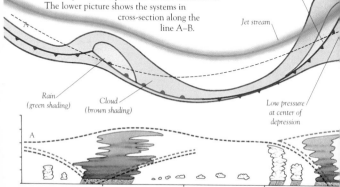

Cold front

Jet stream

Rain (green shading)

Cloud (brown shading)

Low pressure at center of depression

A

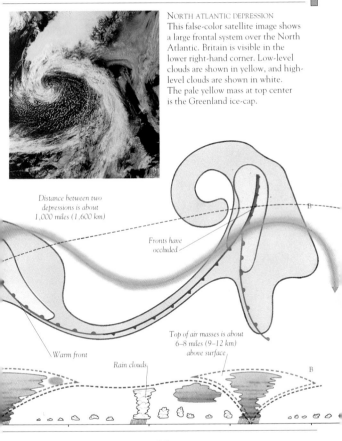

NORTH ATLANTIC DEPRESSION
This false-color satellite image shows
a large frontal system over the North
Atlantic. Britain is visible in the
lower right-hand corner. Low-level
clouds are shown in yellow, and high-
level clouds are shown in white.
The pale yellow mass at top center
is the Greenland ice-cap.

*Distance between two
depressions is about
1,000 miles (1,600 km)*

*Fronts have
occluded*

Warm front

Rain clouds

*Top of air masses is about
6–8 miles (9–12 km)
above surface*

B

LOCAL WINDS

MOUNTAINS OFTEN PRODUCE their own local winds. Some are the result of large-scale winds being shaped by mountains. Other winds are truly local, and are caused by a daily pattern of airflow up and down valleys. In deserts under hot sunshine, thermals can rise very strongly and produce short-lived whirlwinds or "dust-devils."

VALLEY WINDS
Mountain valleys funnel large-scale winds, greatly increasing their strength.

MOUNTAIN AND VALLEY WINDS

NIGHT

Cool air flows down slopes and valleys

Warm air rises up valley sides

DAY

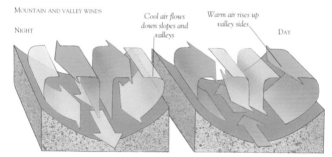

KATABATIC WINDS
These winds occur at night when cool air sinks down mountain slopes and valleys. This is sometimes called katabatic drainage.

ANABATIC WINDS
These occur when sun-warmed air rises and gently flows up mountain slopes and valleys. Cool air flows in to replace it.

DATA BOX: LOCALLY NAMED WINDS

Autan	dry and warm	SW France
Berg	dry and hot	South Africa
Bora	dry and cold	NE Italy
Brickfielder	dry and hot	Australia
Buran	dry and cold	Mongolia
Harmattan	dry and cool	North Africa
Levante	moist and warm	Mediterranean area
Mistral	dry and cold	Rhone Valley, France
Santa Ana	dry and hot	southern California
Sirocco	dry and hot	southern Europe
Tramontana	dry and cold	NE Spain
Zonda	dry and warm	Argentina

WIND FACTS

• When the wind changes in a clockwise direction, it is said to "veer." When the change is counter-clockwise, the wind is said to "back."

• The island of Sumatra has given its name to *sumatras* – gusty winds in the Malacca Strait.

CHINOOK AND FÖHN

As an air mass descends a mountain slope, it is compressed and becomes a warm, dry wind. The effect is most noticeable in spring when these winds can melt snow very quickly. They are called föhn winds in the Alps, and chinook ("snow-eaters") in western North America.

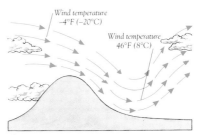

Wind temperature −4°F (−20°C)

Wind temperature 46°F (8°C)

CHINOOK WARMING

HOT AIR SPIRALS

Whirlwinds, "dust-devils," and "sand-devils" are fairly common on sunny days in dry, open country. Intense heating of a patch of ground by the Sun may create a spiraling column of hot air that can reach more than 330 ft (100 m) in height. Lightweight material, such as sand or dust, is lifted up and briefly whirled around. Whirlwinds rarely last more than a few minutes, after which the air column gently collapses.

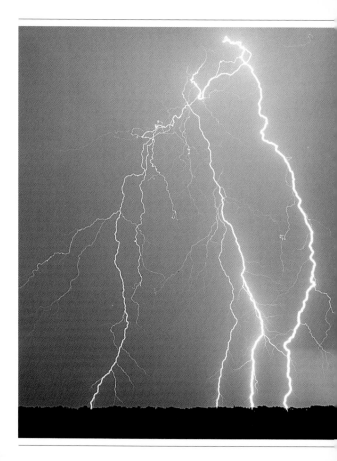

THUNDERSTORMS

STORM CLOUDS

THE MOST POWERFUL of everyday
weather events, thunderstorms
can bring heavy rain, lightning,
hail, and, sometimes, tornadoes.
During a thunderstorm, the sky
is dominated by a towering,
anvil-topped cumulonimbus
cloud. Inside the cloud,
tremendous energy is generated
and unleashed in the form of
swirling upcurrents and jagged
bolts of high-voltage electricity.

TROPICAL THUNDERSTORM
A tropical cumulonimbus
cloud can reach heights of
up to 12 miles (19 km).
The top of the cloud is
sculpted into an anvil
shape by high-level winds.

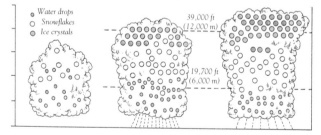

- Water drops
○ Snowflakes
◎ Ice crystals

39,000 ft
(12,000 m)

19,700 ft
(6,000 m)

DEVELOPMENT
Within a cumulonimbus
cloud, water droplets and
snowflakes are carried
upward by air currents,
and raindrops form.

MATURITY
Heavy rain falls at the
surface. Ice particles
collect near the cloud-top,
where temperatures may
reach –68°F (–50°C).

DISSIPATION
The upward air currents
are exhausted, and are
replaced by strong
downdrafts. Light rain
falls at the surface.

INSIDE A STORM CLOUD

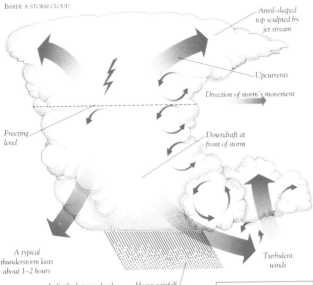

Anvil-shaped
top sculpted by
jet stream

Upcurrents

Direction of storm's movement

Freezing
level

Downdraft at
front of storm

A typical
thunderstorm lasts
about 1–2 hours

Turbulent
winds

Individual storm cloud
measures 1.5–5 miles
(2–8 km) across

Heavy rainfall
and often hail

ATMOSPHERIC POWERHOUSE

A storm cloud receives large amounts of heat energy as water vapor first condenses, and then freezes inside the cloud. The heat energy creates powerful rising air currents that swirl upward to the tropopause. Cool, descending air currents produce strong downdrafts at the front of the storm. After the storm has spent its energy, the rising currents die away, and downdrafts break up the cloud.

THUNDERSTORM FACTS

• At any particular moment in time, there are approximately 1,800 thunderstorms occurring in the Earth's atmosphere.

• A typical flash of fork lightning lasts for about 0.2 seconds.

LIGHTNING

PURE ENERGY unleashed from the skies, lightning is the most exciting and dramatic form of weather. Inside a thundercloud, an enormous electrical charge slowly builds up. The charge is then discharged in a blinding flash, as lightning zigzags between ground and cloud.

RIVEN SKY
Multiple flashes of fork lightning illuminate the evening sky over the city of Lucerne, Switzerland.

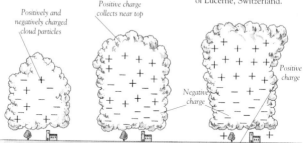

Positively and negatively charged cloud particles

Positive charge collects near top

Positive charge

Negative charge

GENERATION
Inside a thundercloud, electrical charges are produced by countless collisions between ice crystals and hailstones. The cloud particles become electrified.

SEPARATION
The charged particles separate, with positive charge accumulating near the top of the cloud, while the bottom of the cloud becomes predominantly negative.

SHADOW CHARGE
The negative charge at the base of the cloud induces a positive "shadow" charge in the ground beneath.

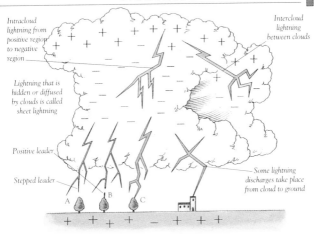

Intracloud lightning from positive region to negative region

Intercloud lightning between clouds

Lightning that is hidden or diffused by clouds is called sheet lightning

Positive leader

Stepped leader

Some lightning discharges take place from cloud to ground

A B C

A   A weak spark (the stepped leader) reaches down from the cloud

B   A positive leader rises to meet it

C   The main discharge (called the return stroke) takes place from ground to cloud along the channel created by the two leaders

LIGHTNING STRIKE

Air around the discharge channel is heated to about 55,000°F (30,000°C). The sound of thunder is made by heated air expanding very rapidly and producing shockwaves. Thunder rumbles because of the timelag between shockwaves from different parts of the discharge channel.

BLOWN APART

An oak tree lies shattered by lightning. A typical discharge delivers about 1.5 million volts. Much of this electrical energy is converted into heat energy. Although the high temperatures last only a few millionths of a second, they are sufficient to vaporize the fluids in a tree trunk, causing it to explode.

TORNADOES

A FULLY-DEVELOPED TORNADO is a violent and terrifying event. A tornado is a high-speed vortex (spiral) or funnel of winds formed by the strong air currents within a storm cloud. Wherever the end of the vortex touches the ground, it creates a path of concentrated destruction that has no equal in nature.

Very low pressure at center of vortex

Vortex darkens as it picks up material from ground

PLAINS DANGER
The most powerful tornadoes occur on the open plains of the US and China. Near the core of a tornado, winds may spiral around at more than 300 mph (480 km/h).

Destruction caused by very rapid changes in pressure

STORM BORN
Tornadoes develop near the boundary between the upcurrents and downdrafts in a storm cloud. A "funnel-cloud" develops first, and this may then extend down to ground level.

Top of tornado
remains inside
storm cloud

Most tornadoes are
less than 200 yd
(200 m) across

A tornado may travel
more than 124 miles
(200 km) across the
land surface

TRAIL OF DESTRUCTION

Most tornadoes leave behind a highly visible trail of destruction, which is usually quite narrow. In this picture of a tornado-stricken Kentucky town, some houses are literally blown apart, while others appear to be untouched.

TUBE OF WATER

Waterspouts are tornado-like vortices that form over water rather than over land. They tend to have much less energy than tornadoes, and are usually confined to shallow, inshore waters during the warmer seasons.

TORNADO FACTS

• The United States has an average of 750 tornadoes per year. The peak months are April, May, and June.

• The fastest-spinning tornadoes often split into multiple smaller tornadoes.

• In November 1981, Britain had a freak outbreak of 102 small tornadoes.

HAIL

ALSO PRODUCED BY thunderstorms, hail is precipitation in the form of pellets of solid ice. Whirled around inside a storm cloud, hailstones can grow dangerously large before they fall.

Each trip through the cloud adds a new layer of ice

Upcurrents repeatedly carry hailstones to the top of the cloud

Hailstones may also collide and stick together

STORM-MADE
Ice pellets falling from the top of the cloud collect a film of moisture as they descend. The moisture freezes when the pellets are carried back to the top by upcurrents. As this process is repeated, the hailstones grow in size.

When a hailstone becomes too heavy for the upcurrents to support, it falls to the ground

Irregular "horns" sometimes form on large hailstones

Spherical core has "onion skin" layers

LAYERS OF A HAILSTONE

When sliced in half and viewed in a laboratory under polarized light, a hailstone reveals its layered structure. Each ice layer represents one trip from the bottom of the cloud to the top and back. While it remains small, the hailstone is almost spherical. As it grows larger, it becomes more irregular in shape.

UNGUIDED MISSILE

Large hailstones are one of the most dangerous weather hazards. Although most are smaller than 1 in (2.5 cm) in diameter, some are as large as tennis balls or even larger. The giant hailstone pictured here fell on Coffeyville, Kansas, in September 1970. It measured 17 in (43 cm) across and weighed 1.7 lb (0.75 kg).

CROP DAMAGE

Hail is one of the worst weather hazards faced by farmers. A sudden summer thunderstorm may unleash a shower of hailstones that can devastate entire fields in a few minutes. Bruised, battered, and beaten flat by the hail, the crops are unharvestable.

HAIL FACTS

• By scientific definition, a hailstone must be at least 0.2 in (5 mm) across.

• Soft hail (also called graupel or snow pellets) consists of roughly spherical particles of opaque ice up to 0.2 in (5 mm) in diameter.

EXTREME WEATHER

HURRICANES

TROPICAL STORMS are the most
powerful of all weather systems,
with wind speeds up to 200 mph
(350 km/h). Called hurricanes
in the Atlantic and eastern
Pacific, cyclones in the Indian
Ocean, and typhoons in the
northwest Pacific, these storms
are characterized by a towering
ring-wall of clouds.

OVERHEAD VIEW
This photograph, taken
from orbit, of Hurricane
Elena clearly shows the "eye"
at the center of the storm.

Curved track

Hurricanes do
not form in the
south Atlantic

STORM TRACKS
This map shows the areas
most affected by tropical storms. The arrows show
the tracks followed by typical storms. Individual
tracks are curved because of "steering" by high-
level winds (jet stream).

Tropical storms form
some distance north or
south of the equator

Dry air descends

High-level winds spiral outward

Whole storm moves in direction of high-level winds

Spiraling bands of wind and rain in ring-wall

Cloud walls fed by water vapor from sea

Warm, moist air drawn in

ROTATING STORM

A hurricane is a massive heat engine powered by heat energy released by the condensation of water vapor. High-speed winds spiral around a calm low-pressure "eye." The clouds in the ring-wall can reach 9 miles (15 km) in height.

STORM SURGE

The intense low pressure at the eye of a hurricane can combine with the effect of strong winds to raise the ocean surface by 23–40 ft (7–12 m). This effect is called a storm surge, and it may cause serious flood damage on low-lying coastlines.

HURRICANE FACTS

• Hurricanes and other tropical storms require a sea-surface temperature of at least 80°F (27°C) in order to form and develop.

• The lowest sea-level pressure ever recorded (15% lower than normal) was in the eye of Typhoon Tip over the Pacific Ocean on October 12, 1979.

TRACKING THE DAMAGE

A TROPICAL STORM is only classified as a hurricane if it has sustained wind speeds of 73 mph (118 km/h). Once it has been classified, it is watched very closely because of its potential to cause death and destruction. Today, satellites enable scientists to monitor the progress of a hurricane.

WITHOUT WARNING
Before the introduction of modern equipment, the only warning of a hurricane's approach was an unexpected increase in wind speed.

SATELLITE IMAGE:
HURRICANE GILBERT
SEPTEMBER 14, 1988

SEPTEMBER 15

"Eye" of hurricane

Yucatan Peninsula

HURRICANE GILBERT
Gilbert was officially declared a hurricane on September 10. Four days later it crossed the Yucatan Peninsula in southern Mexico.

SEPTEMBER 15
Gilbert had a force 5 rating (the highest possible rating for a hurricane) when it struck the Yucatan. As it crossed the peninsula, it began to lose energy and was downgraded to a force 3 rating. It then headed toward the US.

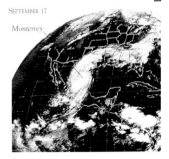

Monterrey

SEPTEMBER 16
Once back over warm tropical waters Gilbert stopped losing energy, and stayed at force 3. However, with wind speeds reaching 124 mph (200 km/h), the hurricane was still a considerable threat to life and property.

Spiral cloud formation is beginning to unwind as Gilbert loses energy

SEPTEMBER 16

SEPTEMBER 17
Gilbert's course took it back across the Mexican coastline. A 7-foot (2-meter) storm surge caused extensive damage. As it moved inland, the storm lost more energy. When it reached the city of Monterrey, winds had slowed to 75 mph (120 km/h). Floods caused by 4 in (10 cm) of rain drowned 200 people.

WIPEOUT
The town of Darwin in northern Australia was devastated by Cyclone Tracy. Like many towns in the tropical climate region, most of the buildings were of fairly lightweight construction. As a result, they were easily blown apart by hurricane-force winds.

HURRICANE FACTS
• The systematic naming of hurricanes began during WWII. Until the 1970s, only female names were used. Since then, male and female names have been used alternately.

• Each year about 35 tropical storms reach hurricane status.

FLOODS

WHEN WATER INVADES an area of land, flooding occurs. Some floods are the result of sudden and torrential rain in the local area, while others are caused by snowmelt or rainfall over a wide area. Flooding also occurs when a river bursts its banks, or the sea surges over a coastline.

SURGE SHELTER
Along some stretches of the Bangladeshi coast, strong concrete shelters have been built to give people protection against storm surge flooding.

Heavy rainfall causes the level of streams and rivers to rise

Downstream, the main river cannot hold all the water pouring in from rain-swollen tributaries

RIVER FLOODS
Prolonged rain can produce a slow-acting river flood as water from upstream tributaries gradually builds up. Areas near to the confluence (junction) of major tributaries are especially vulnerable to this type of flooding.

Many large rivers are bordered by a floodplain that is subject to regular flooding

SWOLLEN RIVER

This false-color image was obtained by a Landsat satellite during the 1993 flooding of the Mississippi and Missouri rivers in the US. The city of St. Louis is the purple area at bottom center. The Mississippi River flows top left to bottom right, and the Missouri River flows from the left, joining midway down the image. Blue and black coloring show the extent of the flooded area.

WATER DAMAGE

Flood water from a burst river bank flows through the streets of an English town. One of the worst aspects of flood damage is the contamination of drinking-water supplies by sewage and other waste materials.

DATA BOX: NOTABLE FLOODS		
Type	Date and location	Fatalities
Storm surge	1970 Bay of Bengal	250,000+
Storm surge	1900 Galveston, Texas	7,200
Dam failure	1889 Johnstown, New York	2,100
River flood	1913 Ohio River	467
Flash flood	1974 Big Thompson Canyon, Colorado	150
Tsunami	1883 Krakatau	36,000

FLOOD FACT

• The effects of the Krakatau tsunami (a destructive surge wave produced by a volcanic eruption or earthquake), which originated near Java, were felt as far away as San Francisco, and ports on the English Channel.

DROUGHT

SHORTAGE OF WATER, drought is a widespread problem. Areas that normally receive an adequate supply of water are the ones hardest hit by drought. The basic cause of all droughts is inadequate rainfall, often prolonged over a period of several years.

FAILING VEGETATION
In the Australian outback, low rainfall has caused mineral salts, which are harmful to vegetation, to build up in the soil.

AREAS WHICH RECEIVE INSUFFICIENT PRECIPITATION FOR NATURAL VEGETATION OR CROPS TO THRIVE

INADEQUATE RAINFALL
This map shows the areas of the world that do not receive enough rainfall. Irrigation is necessary for agriculture, and drought is a constant threat.

DATA BOX: NOTABLE DROUGHTS

Date	Location	
1910–14	Sahel	The region south of the
1940–44	Sahel	Sahara Desert has suffered
1972–75	Sahel	from persistent drought
1982–85	Sahel	for most of this century.
1933–37	US	Created the "Dust Bowl"
1962–66	US	Affected northeastern states
1977	US	Water rationed in California
1965–67	India	1.5 million people died
1967–69	Australia	Resulted in many bush fires
1975–76	England	Below 50% average rainfall

DROUGHT FACTS

• There is no universally accepted definition of drought, and scientific literature contains at least 150 different definitions.

• In July and August 1986, the US suffered a combined drought and heat-wave that killed 48 people.

Cloudless skies and no rain

Descending air currents from high-pressure system

BLOCKING HIGH
In the midlatitudes, a short-term drought may be caused by a "blocking high." A high-pressure system may remain stationary over an area of land for several weeks. The high pressure blocks the passage of low-pressure systems that bring rain. The result is weeks of drought.

Path of low-pressure systems diverted by "blocking high"

SUN-CRACKED LAKE BED

BLIZZARDS AND SANDSTORMS

WINDBLOWN PARTICLES of snow and sand are a normal part of weather in polar and desert regions. In remote areas, they cause little disruption. However, when blizzards and sandstorms occur in highly populated areas, they can cause chaos. Visibility is greatly reduced, and most forms of transportation are paralyzed.

BLIZZARD
A blizzard is snow blown by winds that have an average speed of at least 32 mph (52 km/h).

SNOW MOVEMENT

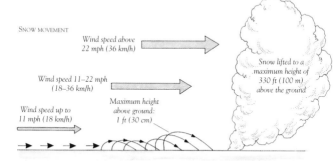

Wind speed above 22 mph (36 km/h)

Snow lifted to a maximum height of 330 ft (100 m) above the ground

Wind speed 11–22 mph (18–36 km/h)

Wind speed up to 11 mph (18 km/h)

Maximum height above ground: 1 ft (30 cm)

SNOW CREEP
Under gentle winds, snow particles roll along the ground, rising no more than 1 in (2.5 cm) above the surface.

SALTATION
Under moderate winds, snow particles jump and bounce along the ground in a form of movement called saltation.

TURBULENT DIFFUSION
In strong winds, the wind has enough force to lift fallen snow back into the air in a process called turbulent diffusion.

SANDSTORM

A sandstorm darkens the sky in sub-Saharan Africa. There are two types of storm. A small sandstorm (*haboob*) is formed by the downdraft winds of a thunderstorm. A large sandstorm (*khamsin*) is formed by strong winds that blow for several days.

DUST STORM

With dramatic suddenness, a dust storm sweeps across a Canadian airport. Dust particles are smaller and lighter than sand and are lifted into the atmosphere more easily. This particular storm was raised by the strong winds at the leading edge of a cold front.

DATA BOX: WINDCHILL EFFECT

Air temperature	Wind speed 10 mph (6 km/h)	20 mph (32 km/h)
32°F (0°C)	27°F (−3°C)	21°F (−6°C)
28°F (−2°C)	23°F (−5°C)	15°F (−9°C)
24°F (−4°C)	19°F (−7°C)	10°F (−12°C)
20°F (−7°C)	14°F (−10°C)	5°F (−15°C)
16°F (−9°C)	10°F (−12°C)	0°F (−19°C)
12°F (−12°C)	6°F (−14°C)	−5°F (−20°C)
8°F (−14°C)	1°F (−17°C)	−11°F (−24°C)
4°F (−16°C)	−3°F (−19°C)	−16°F (−27°C)

FREEZING RAIN

Rain falling through very cold air, or onto cold objects, can freeze into a coating of clear ice. This is also known as glaze.

BY SEA AND AIR

WEATHER CREATES SPECIAL perils for ships and aircraft. At sea, waves and swell produced by storms are the major hazards. In the air, the main dangers are hailstones and abrupt changes in wind velocity (both of which are also produced by storms). Thick fog, which can conceal coastlines and runways, is another common hazard.

LIGHT AND SOUND
Lighthouses, built on the coast or on offshore rocks, use both light and sound to warn ships of fog. The sound of a lighthouse foghorn can be heard for about 20 miles (30 km) over water.

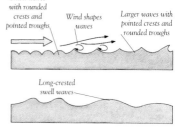

Small waves with rounded crests and pointed troughs

Wind shapes waves

Larger waves with pointed crests and rounded troughs

Long-crested swell waves

WAVES AND SWELL
Wind blowing gently over a water surface produces small, rounded waves. As the wind speed increases, the waves become pointed. Once produced, the waves travel great distances as rounded swell waves.

STORM WAVES
A storm can transform the sea's surface into an unpredictable roller-coaster ride. Waves of up to 60 ft (18 m) are fairly common. The largest documented wave measured 112 ft (34 m) in height.

DOWNBURSTER

Sudden changes in wind velocity are one of the most dangerous hazards facing aircraft that are coming in to land. A thunderstorm can produce unexpected vertical "downbursts" of 60 mph (96 km/h) or more. Flying through a downburst may cause the aircraft to crash.

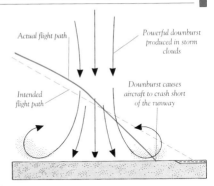

Actual flight path

Powerful downburst produced in storm clouds

Intended flight path

Downburst causes aircraft to crash short of the runway

BATTERED NOSE

Flying through a hailstorm battered and bent the front of this passenger aircraft. All hailstones more than 0.5 in (1.2 cm) in diameter can damage an aircraft, although only large hailstones can cause this much damage. Pilots are trained to avoid the dangers of hail by flying around, rather than beneath, storm clouds.

FOG DISPERSAL

At Orly Airport, Paris, France, jet engines of the Turboclair system are mounted in a series of pits alongside the main runway. When fog reduces visibility to hazardous limits, the system is switched on. Hot air from the jet-engines evaporates the fog for clear takeoffs and landings.

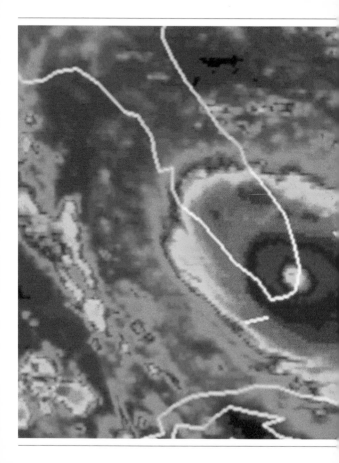

MEASURING AND MAPPING

MEASURING PRESSURE

VARIATIONS IN air pressure, in space and in time, are vitally important to understanding how the weather machine works. Instruments called barometers are used for measuring pressure. The readings obtained can then be plotted on a map to produce a pressure chart.

PRESSURE CLOCK
This aneroid barometer contains a partial vacuum in a specially constructed metal box. Changes in air pressure affect the shape of the box and move the pointer around the dial to indicate the pressure.

Rises or falls in pressure are recorded on a roll of paper

BAROGRAPH
This instrument is composed of an aneroid barometer with a pen instead of a pointer. The pen rests against a slowly revolving drum. The pen marks a roll of paper on the drum. Barographs are particularly important for providing a continuous record of air pressure.

PRESSURE FACTS

• The average air pressure at sea level over the whole planet is 1013.2 millibars (or 29.92 in of mercury).

• The highest recorded air pressure, adjusted to sea level, was 1083.8 millibars (or 32 in of mercury) at Agata, Siberia, on December 31, 1968.

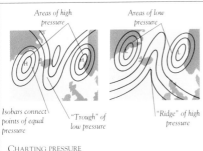

Areas of high pressure

Areas of low pressure

19TH-CENTURY MERCURY BAROMETER

Isobars connect points of equal pressure

"Trough" of low pressure

"Ridge" of high pressure

CHARTING PRESSURE
Points on a map that have the same air pressure are connected by lines known as isobars. By studying the patterns shown by isobars, forecasters can make predictions about how the weather will develop.

VACUUM DISCOVERY
The Italian scientist Evangelista Torricelli (1608–47) made the first barometer in 1644 by supporting a column of mercury inside a glass tube. The height of the column varies according to the air pressure.

MERCURY BAROMETER
Some barometers consist of a closed-off glass tube that is inverted in a pool of mercury. The higher the atmospheric pressure, the farther the mercury is forced up the tube. This distance, or height, is measured in inches or millimeters. Atmospheric pressure is also measured in millibars. One millibar is equal to 100 pascals (1 hectopascal).

Height of mercury shows air pressure

MEASURING WIND

AIR IN MOTION, wind has both
speed and direction. At the
Earth's surface, wind is greatly
affected by friction with the land
or water beneath. For this reason,
wind is normally measured at a
height of 33 feet (10 meters).

WIND DIRECTION
Wind vanes are a traditional
method of indicating the
wind's direction.

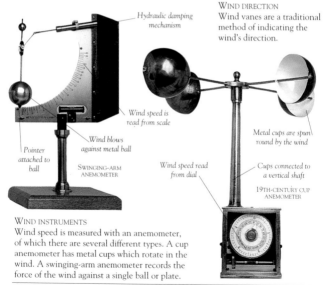

*Hydraulic damping
mechanism*

*Wind speed is
read from scale*

*Metal cups are spun
round by the wind*

*Wind blows
against metal ball*

*Pointer
attached to
ball*

SWINGING-ARM
ANEMOMETER

*Wind speed read
from dial*

*Cups connected to
a vertical shaft*

19TH-CENTURY CUP
ANEMOMETER

WIND INSTRUMENTS
Wind speed is measured with an anemometer,
of which there are several different types. A cup
anemometer has metal cups which rotate in the
wind. A swinging-arm anemometer records the
force of the wind against a single ball or plate.

Force 1:
2 mph (3 km/h)
smoke drifts

Force 2:
5 mph (9 km/h)
leaves rustle

VISIBLE SIGNS

Wind speed is sometimes given according to the Beaufort Scale which was intended for use at sea when no accurate instruments were available. Today, the Beaufort Scale is mainly used to report weather at sea, a "force 9 gale," for example. On land, various indicators, such as the movement of smoke or branches, enable the wind speed to be estimated with reasonable accuracy.

Force 3:
10 mph
(15 km/h)
flags flutter

Force 4: 15 mph (25 km/h)
small branches move

Force 5: 21 mph (35 km/h)
small trees sway

Force 6: 28 mph (45 km/h)
large branches move

Force 7:
35 mph
(56 km/h)
whole trees
sway

Force 9: 50 mph (81 km/h)
branches break

Force 8:
43 mph (68 km/h)
twigs break

WIND FACTS

• The strongest winds ever measured (excluding tornadoes) were gusts of 231 mph (372 km/h) at Mount Washington, New Hampshire, on April 12, 1934.

• The first official hurricane warning was issued in 1847 by William Reid, the British governor of Barbados.

Force 10:
59 mph (94 km/h)
trees blow down

Force 11:
69 mph (110 km/h)
serious damage

Force 12:
74 mph (118 km/h)
hurricane damage

MEASURING RAIN

THE QUANTITY OF rainfall is not measured directly by volume or weight. Rain is measured in the same way as water on the Earth's surface, in units of depth. Rain falling at any particular point is treated as though it piles up on the ground instead of soaking in.

HOW MUCH RAIN?
Rainfall figures are best thought of as fairly reliable estimates. Factors such as wind speed make accurate measurement very difficult.

RAIN GAUGE

Funnel and protective can are often made of copper

RAIN GAUGE
Falling raindrops are collected before they reach the ground. Rain falls into a steep-sided funnel, which drains into a collecting bottle. Any rain that has been collected is measured in a separate cylinder, which has a specially marked scale. The measuring scale takes into account the area of the top of the funnel, so that a rainfall figure per unit area can be obtained.

Measuring cylinder with graduated scale

DATA BOX: MAXIMUM RAINFALL RECORDS		
1 min	1.1 in (3.1 cm)	Unionville, Mo.
8 min	5 in (12.5 cm)	Fussen, Germany
15 min	7.8 in (19.8 cm)	Plumb Point, Jamaica
20 min	8 in (20.4 cm)	De Arges, Romania
42 min	12 in (30.5 cm)	Holt, Mo.
9 hr	44 in (111.8 cm)	La Réunion (island)
24 hr	73.6 in (187 cm)	La Réunion
2 days	98 in (248.9 cm)	La Réunion
8 days	163 in (414 cm)	La Réunion
1 month	366 in (929.6 cm)	Cherrapunji, India

RAIN FACTS

• A snowfall of 10 in (25 cm) is equivalent to approximately 1 in (2.5 cm) of rainfall.

• On the upper slopes of Mt. Wai-ale-ale, Hawaii, rain falls on average on 335 days per year.

AUTOMATIC MEASUREMENT
In remote locations it is not possible to check an ordinary rain gauge every day. A bucket-siphon rain gauge takes its own measurement each day, and then empties the collecting bottle to be ready for the next rainfall. The amounts collected are automatically recorded on a paper roll.

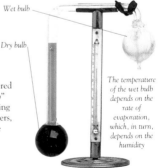

Wet bulb

Dry bulb

The temperature of the wet bulb depends on the rate of evaporation, which, in turn, depends on the humidity

HUMIDITY
The amount of water vapor in air is measured with a hygrometer. This "wet and dry bulb" hygrometer measures humidity by comparing the temperatures given by two thermometers, one of which is wrapped in wet cloth. The drier (less humid) the air, the greater the temperature difference.

MEASURING SUN

THE DURATION and intensity of
sunlight are only a part of
measuring the Sun. Equally
important are the temperatures
that result from solar heating (or
the lack of it), and the amount of
cloud cover that
may obscure
the Sun.

OBSCURED BY CLOUDS
During the day, the Sun is
always shining. The amount
of sunshine reaching the
ground, however, depends
on the amount and
duration of any cloud cover.

SUNSHINE RECORDER

*Glass sphere
concentrates sunlight
like a magnifying glass*

*Cardboard record strip is
graduated in hours*

SUNSHINE RECORDER
A simple but effective daily
sunshine recorder consists of
a sphere of optical-quality
glass fixed in a suitable stand.
Sunlight falling on the recorder is
concentrated by the glass sphere so that it
burns a line across a cardboard strip attached to the stand. The amount and
timing of sunshine can be obtained by
examining the burned line. The more
sunshine there is, the longer the line.

*Cardboard is specially
treated so that it
cannot catch fire*

WEATHER FACTS

• The cloudiest part of the world is around latitude 60°S from December to February, when cloud cover averages 80% or more.

• The longest continuous record of sunshine has been maintained at Kew, a district of London, England.

• The earliest known weather journal was kept in Latin between 1337 and 1344.

CLOUDINESS

The amount of cloud cover is usually given in units called oktas. Each okta represents one eighth of the sky covered by cloud.

Clear sky

1 okta

2 oktas

3 oktas

4 oktas

5 oktas

6 oktas

7 oktas

Overcast

This scale records the minimum temperature

Tiny metal pointers inside the thermometer tube mark the highest and lowest temperatures

MAXIMUM AND MINIMUM

Some weather stations use a maximum and minimum thermometer to record the highest and lowest temperatures during a particular time period, usually one day.

This scale records the maximum temperature

CELSIUS

The Swedish astronomer Anders Celsius (1701-44) is credited with devising a centigrade temperature scale which was divided into 100 degrees between the freezing point and the boiling point of water.

SYNOPTIC CHARTS

THE STANDARD weather map is known as a synoptic chart. It shows a detailed picture of the weather at a particular time. The chart is compiled from weather reports from many different weather stations.

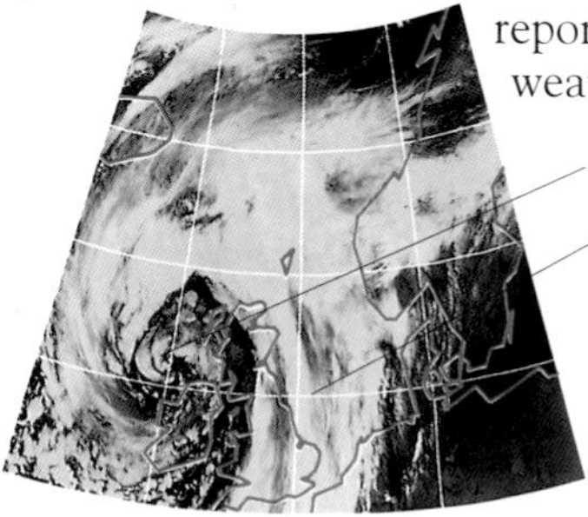

Center of depression (area of lowest pressure)

Thick cloud at the leading edge of the depression

Isobars drawn at 8-millibar intervals

Warm front

SATELLITE PHOTOGRAPH

NORTHWEST ATLANTIC
18.00 HRS
JANUARY 17, 1995
This satellite photograph and the synoptic chart both show the same thing, a depression to the west of Britain. The chart shows more detailed information.

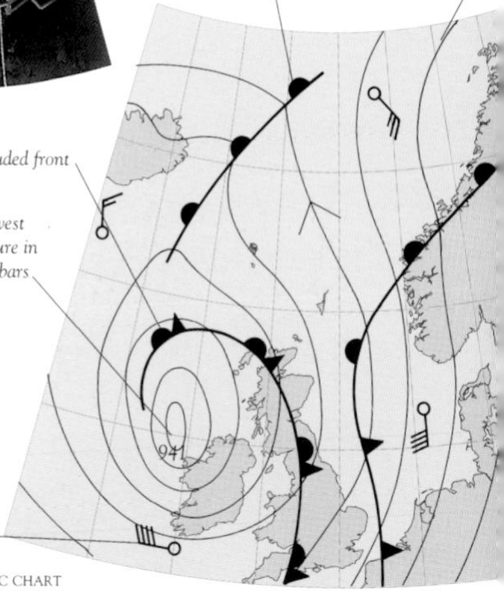

Occluded front

Lowest pressure in millibars

Indicates wind speeds of about 45–50 mph (72–80 km/h)

SYNOPTIC CHART

SOME OF THE WEATHER SYMBOLS USED ON SYNOPTIC CHARTS

• •	SLIGHT RAIN, CONTINUOUS	••••	MODERATE RAIN, CONTINUOUS	•••••	HEAVY RAIN, CONTINUOUS
❟	DRIZZLE	✳	SNOW	△	HAIL
▽	SHOWERS	▽̇	MODERATE OR HEAVY RAIN SHOWERS	▲▽	SLIGHT SHOWERS OF HAIL
•|	PRECIPITATION DURING LAST HOUR	≡	FOG	�RⳐ	THUNDERSTORM
◣◣◣	COLD FRONT AT SURFACE	⬤⬤⬤	WARM FRONT AT SURFACE	◣⬤◣	OCCLUDED FRONT

WIND SPEED   *Each full feather represents about 10 mph (16 km/h)*

Tail shows wind direction

CALM ◯ ◯ ◯ ◯ ◯ ◯ ◯ ◯ ◯ GALES

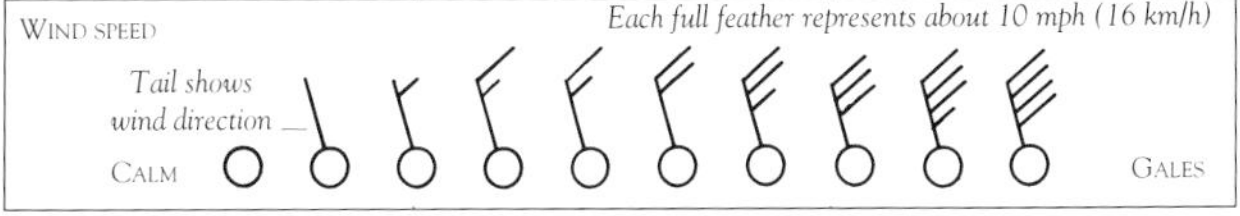

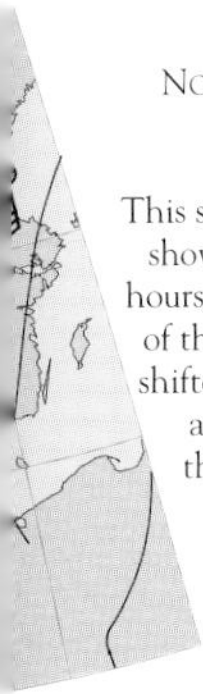

Center of depression over Iceland

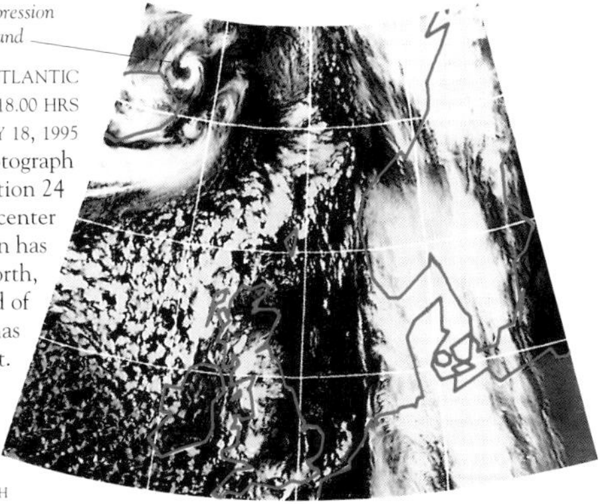

NORTHWEST ATLANTIC
18.00 HRS
JANUARY 18, 1995

This satellite photograph shows the situation 24 hours later. The center of the depression has shifted to the north, and the band of thick cloud has moved east.

SATELLITE PHOTOGRAPH

OTHER MAPS

WEATHER MAPS must serve a variety of purposes, and synoptic charts are not suitable for every occasion. Television forecasters, for example, often show greatly simplified maps with pictorial symbols. In the Tropics, maps with streamlines are more useful than maps with isobars. Special maps are also produced by those studying a particular aspect of weather, such as lightning.

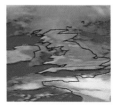

TV PRESENTATION
A computer-generated display often accompanies a weather summary on television. This display shows precipitation over Britain and France.

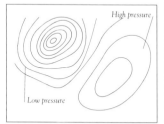

TROPICAL WEATHER
In tropical regions, and especially near the equator, isobars do not give a particularly helpful picture. This map shows a low-pressure area on the left, and a high-pressure area on the right.

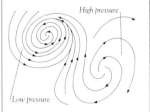

STREAMLINE VIEW
This map shows the same tropical weather. The streamlines (lines that follow the direction of airflow) give a clearer picture of the winds that spiral out from the high and into the low.

SIGWX
18.00 HRS
JANUARY 17,
1995

SIGNIFICANT MAPS
Maps showing significant weather effects (abbreviated as SIGWX) only show weather that may affect flying conditions. SIGWX maps are usually issued four times per day. Rain, hail, storms, and other potential hazards are clearly marked by the same symbols that are used on synoptic charts.

SIGWX
18.00 HRS
JANUARY 18,
1995

RAPID CHANGE
In Britain, as in many other countries, SIGWX charts are especially important because weather conditions change so frequently. This map and the one above were drawn just 24 hours apart, yet they show two very different sets of weather circumstances from a pilot's viewpoint.

DISPLAY LIGHTNING
This on-screen display at the headquarters of the US National Lightning Detection Network shows thunderstorm activity during five hours on the night of April 7, 1991. The display is color-coded according to the timing of each lightning strike recorded by the network.

FORECASTING

TRADITIONAL METHODS

HUMAN ACTIVITY is very closely linked to the weather, and being able to predict the weather gives people an advantage. Wherever humans have settled, they have begun to accumulate a store of weather knowledge. This traditional lore is often in the form of short rhymes.

FORECASTING CONES
Cones open and close according to the humidity of the air. An open cone is supposed to mean dry weather, and a closed cone indicates damp weather.

SEAWEED INDICATOR
Marine algae (seaweed) is a favorite tool of traditional forecasters. Like needleleaf cones, seaweed responds to changes in humidity. The lower the humidity, the more likely it is to be dry the next day.

Dry seaweed indicates dry weather

OAK AND ASH TREES

Ash leaf before the oak,
Then we shall have a summer soak;
Oak leaf before the ash,
The summer comes with nary a splash.
In the US, this rhyme is supposed
to predict the summer weather on
the basis of which tree comes
into leaf first, the oak or the ash.
Such lore is based on years of
observation, and may sometimes
be correct. However, it is likely to
be wrong as often as it is right.

ASH TREE IN
FULL LEAF

The woman outside indicates low
humidity and (in theory) dry weather

WEATHER-HOUSE

The traditional European weather-
house is in fact a simple version of a
hair hygrometer. The figures of a man
and a woman are mounted on a
platform suspended by a hair. Changes
in humidity cause either the man or
woman to emerge from the house.

RED SKY AT NIGHT

Red sky at night
Sailor's delight
Red sky in the morning
Sailor's warning
The redness of the sky depends on the
amount of water vapor in the air.
In the US, where weather comes from
the west, a red dawn suggests that wet
weather is approaching.

GATHERING INFORMATION

MUCH OF THE INFORMATION
used by forecasters is obtained
from small land-based weather
stations. Many of these are
now automated, although
some still have to be visited,
and readings copied down by
hand. Additional information
is provided by aircraft, ships,
buoys, and balloons.

BALLOON LAUNCH
Radiosonde weather
balloons are released twice
a day in many countries.

WEATHER INSTRUMENTS HOUSED IN A STEVENSON SCREEN

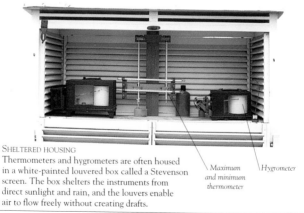

SHELTERED HOUSING
Thermometers and hygrometers are often housed
in a white-painted louvered box called a Stevenson
screen. The box shelters the instruments from
direct sunlight and rain, and the louvers enable
air to flow freely without creating drafts.

Maximum
and minimum
thermometer

Hygrometer

Instruments use lasers to photograph cloud particles

WEATHER AIRCRAFT
Specially equipped aircraft are used to obtain temperature and humidity readings, and to take pictures of cloud particles.

Radar for measuring clouds

RADIOSONDES
Before the first weather satellites were put into orbit, weather balloons were the only means of obtaining information about the upper atmosphere. Balloons are still used today, and carry radiosonde equipment that transmits information to the ground.

Helium-filled balloon

Solar panel provides energy

OCEAN WATCH
Loaded with sensitive instruments, weather buoys drift with the ocean currents and help complete the global weather picture.

Vanes detect wind direction

FULLY AUTOMATIC
Modern weather stations are fully automated installations, often powered by solar energy. Readings are relayed to forecasting centers by communications satellites.

SATELLITES

"EYES IN THE SKY" have given scientists a better view of the weather, and have revolutionized their understanding of weather processes. Forecasts are now much more accurate, thanks to the information provided by remote-sensing instruments aboard Earth-orbiting satellites.

ON-SCREEN INFORMATION
Readings from instruments aboard satellites are often displayed in visual form on TV screens.

ERS-1 POLAR ORBITING
WEATHER SATELLITE
(PRELAUNCH CONFIGURATION)

Radar altimeter
measures wave height
and sea-ice thickness

Active microwave
radar
(antenna folded)

Antenna for
communicating
with Earth

Radiometer
measures sea
temperature

SATELLITE SCANS
There are two main types of weather satellite. Geostationary satellites remain above the same point on the Earth's surface, and can scan almost half the planet every 30 minutes. Those in polar orbits can scan a different area every two hours or so.

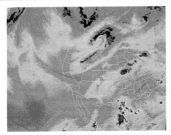

COLOR-CODED MOISTURE
This false-color image of the atmosphere has been color-coded to show the amount of water in the atmosphere above North America and the western Pacific. Blue and green areas represent moisture in the form of clouds, rain, or snow.

WATER VAPOR VISION
This satellite image was obtained with infrared equipment that had been fine-tuned to be sensitive to the water vapor in the Earth's atmosphere. Some large-scale and semipermanent cloud features can be identified.

Subtropical high-pressure region

Subtropical high-pressure region

Clouds in the ITCZ

LOOKING INTO THE EYE
Satellites are not the only form of space exploration that benefits weather scientists. This remarkable photograph, looking vertically down into the eye of Hurricane Emilia, was taken with a hand-held camera by a crewmember aboard the Space Shuttle. The blue color at the center of the picture is the surface of the Pacific Ocean.

GLOBAL VIEWS

WEATHER SATELLITES are the most important of the new remote-sensing "tools" that are now used by meteorologists (weather scientists). A single satellite in polar orbit can cover the whole surface of the Earth in just three days and produce huge amounts of data. There is so much weather data now available that scientists must use powerful computers to reduce the information to a manageable form.

Cloud associated with the Gulf Stream

Cloudless skies over the Australian desert

High-level cloud in the tropical zone

CLOUD COVER
This image shows global cloud cover on a typical July day, as viewed by the US National Oceanic and Atmospheric Administration satellite. Red indicates high-level cloud, green indicates middle-level cloud, and blue indicates low-level cloud. The greater the intensity of coloring, the greater the percentage of cloud cover; with black indicating little or no cloud.

REALISTIC VIEW

This satellite image of Europe was obtained with synthetic aperture radar-mapping equipment that can penetrate cloud cover. The image has been artificially colored to provide a realistic view of the Earth's surface as seen from space. Modern radar equipment is so sensitive that satellites can even measure wind speed.

WAVE HEIGHT

This false-color image shows the wave height of the oceans. Blue represents waves up to 7 ft (2 m), red for waves of about 17 ft (5 m), and yellow for waves of 33 ft (10 m) or more. Note a storm off the coast of South Africa, which caused havoc for shipping in this region.

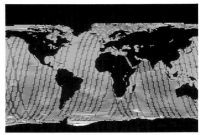

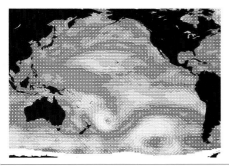

OCEANIC WINDS

This map, produced with satellite data, shows the winds over the Pacific Ocean. The arrows show wind direction and the colors indicate speed, with yellow showing speeds of 35–44 mph (57–70 km/h). Note the storm center to the east of New Zealand.

COMPUTERS

FORECASTING means predicting future weather on the basis of what is happening in the present. Readings from thousands of weather stations, and data and images obtained by satellites, must all be taken into account. Computers are used to process this information and produce reasonably accurate forecasts. Even the most powerful computer cannot predict the weather more than about five days in advance.

SUPERCOMPUTER
This supercomputer in Boulder, Colorado, is used to perform the millions of calculations per second that are necessary to model and predict the world's ever-changing weather.

COMPUTER MODEL
Scientists use computers to create models of the atmosphere. They divide the atmosphere into a gridwork of squares.

GRID SIZE
The model's accuracy depends on the size of the grid. Each square is given a single value for temperature and pressure.

LIMITATIONS
Decreasing the size of the squares increases the number of calculations that have to be made for each forecast.

BUTTERFLY EFFECT

Studying the weather has confronted scientists with the limits of cause and effect. The more closely they examine weather, the more factors they have to take into account. This is often expressed as the "butterfly effect." A single butterfly flapping its wings could provide the initial movement of air that eventually becomes a hurricane.

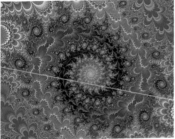

CHAOTIC WEATHER

The mathematics of weather forecasting are very complex. Small differences in initial conditions, such as a half-degree variation in air temperature, can lead to greatly differing results a few days later. This situation is sometimes described as chaotic. Like this spiral design, no matter how closely you look at weather, it is always complex.

DATA BOX: INCREASING COMPUTER SPEED 1965–94		
Year	Number of instructions processed	
1965	1,000,000	per second
1970	2,200,000	per second
1977	5,000,000	per second
1983	8,000,000	per second
1985	15,000,000	per second
1988	23,000,000	per second
1990	47,000,000	per second
1994	62,000,000	per second

FORECASTING FACT

• A typical weather forecasting model divides the globe into 56-mile (90-km) grid squares and takes readings at 19 levels. The 1,187,500 items of data obtained are processed by a computer in less than 10 minutes.

CHANGING WEATHER

LOCAL EFFECTS

PEOPLE CAN DEFINITELY change the weather, at least in some places some of the time. Unfortunately, the changes that people have so far produced have been mostly unintended and undesirable.

ACID RAIN DAMAGE
This forest on the slopes of the Harz mountains in Germany has been ravaged by acid rain.

Nitrogen oxide and sulfur dioxide combine with water to produce dilute sulfuric and nitric acid

Burning fossil fuels (especially coal) produces large quantities of sulfur dioxide gas

Rainwater often contains other pollution as well as dilute acids

ACID RAIN
Some of the pollution emitted by factories and vehicles combines with water in the atmosphere to produce acid rain. In addition to killing many trees where it falls, acid rain enters rivers and lakes, where it kills fish and other aquatic animals.

Vehicle exhausts produce large quantities of nitrogen oxide gas

Layer of warm stagnant air
(pink) trapped between two
layers of cooler air (blue)

Air pollution is trapped
by a temperature
inversion

SMOG

When pollution is trapped near the ground by a temperature inversion, smog can form. Smog is a thick, dirty, poisonous fog. Some of the chemicals in pollution are changed by the action of sunlight to produce an even more dangerous photochemical smog. Controls on vehicle exhaust emissions help reduce smog.

URBAN MISERY

Smog is a growing problem, and cities on every continent are now afflicted by it. Quite apart from the problems caused by reduced visibility, smog is a medical hazard. People suffering from chest illnesses are especially at risk. During the 1950s, smogs killed thousands of Londoners and hospitalized many more.

HAIL LIMITATION

In Russia, rockets loaded with chemicals are sometimes used to "seed" thunderstorms. The chemical seeding can make storm clouds release hail before the hailstones have grown big enough to damage valuable crops.

LOCAL EFFECT FACT

• The city of Los Angeles, California, uses 8.7 million gallons of gasoline, diesel fuel, and aviation fuel each day, and as a result produces more than 12,000 tons (tonnes) of atmospheric pollution every day.

GLOBAL CLIMATE

THE EARTH'S CLIMATE is in a state of continuous, but very slow, change. Less than 15,000 years ago, an ice sheet covered much of Europe and North America. Since then, the global climate has naturally warmed up. Some scientists, however, have recently become concerned that human activity is accelerating the pace of global warming.

AEROSOL GASES
Some aerosols use chemical gases known as chloro-fluorocarbons (CFCs) as a propellant. CFCs collect in the upper atmosphere, where they destroy ozone.

"Hole" of decreased ozone content

OZONE HOLE
In the stratosphere, ozone absorbs ultraviolet (UV) rays that would otherwise be harmful to life. There appears to have been a recent reduction in the amount of ozone. This photograph shows the so-called "hole" in the ozone above Antarctica. An increase in UV radiation could lead to higher surface temperatures and a significantly greater risk of skin cancer in humans.

SHRINKING SEA

This satellite photograph shows the shrinking Aral Sea, a lake on the border between Kazakhstan and Uzbekistan. Much of the water that would normally enter the lake was diverted for irrigation purposes. As a result, the Aral Sea has now shrunk to about half its former size. People who lived along the shores of the lake now find themselves inhabiting an artificially produced desert.

FOREST CLEARANCE

This smoke from a burning rainforest was photographed by a Space Shuttle crew member. Most scientific evidence suggests that the persistent use of such methods to clear large areas of land is changing the Earth's climate. But it is still unclear exactly what will be the result of these changes.

THE FUTURE

This map shows one possible prediction for year 2050. As a combined result of natural and artificial warming, average surface temperatures have increased by a few degrees. The complexities of the global climate and weather machine mean that the increase is unevenly distributed.

No change
+1.8°F (+1°C)
+3.6°F (+2°C)
+5.4°F (+3°C)
+7.2°F (+4°C)

Glossary

AIR
A naturally occurring mixture of gases, chiefly nitrogen and oxygen with small amounts of argon and carbon dioxide. Air also usually contains dust, pollen, and water vapor.

AIR MASS
A body of air with fairly uniform temperature and humidity.

AIR PRESSURE
The force exerted on a horizontal surface by the weight of the air above. Also called atmospheric pressure.

ALBEDO
The measure of the reflectivity of a surface.

ANEMOMETER
An instrument for measuring wind speed.

ANTICYCLONE
A high-pressure weather system; a "high."

ATMOSPHERE
A layer of gases surrounding a planet.

ATMOSPHERIC PRESSURE
See air pressure.

BAROGRAPH
An instrument that provides a continuous record of air pressure.

BAROMETER
An instrument for measuring air pressure.

BLIZZARD
Snow blown by winds with an average speed of at least 32 mph (52 km/h).

CHINOOK
The American term for a dry, downslope wind.

CLIMATE
The prevailing or "normal" pattern of weather at a place, or in a region, averaged over a long period of time.

CLOUD
A structure formed in the lower atmosphere by condensed water vapor or ice particles.

CONDENSATION
The process by which water vapor becomes liquid water.

CONDENSATION NUCLEUS
A microscopic particle of dust or salt, upon which water vapor condenses in the atmosphere.

CONDUCTION
Process of heat transfer through materials and adjoining substances.

CONTINENTALITY
The tendency for the middle regions of continents to have a wider temperature range than coastal areas.

CONVECTION
Process of heat transfer through fluids by means of rising currents.

CORIOLIS FORCE
An effect caused by the Earth's rotation, which causes winds and currents to follow a curved path across the Earth's surface.

CYCLONE
The name used for a hurricane in the Indian Ocean and Western Pacific. Also refers to any low-pressure weather system.

DEPRESSION
A low-pressure weather system; a "low." Also called a cyclone.

DESERT
An area, either hot or cold, where the annual precipitation is less than 10 in (25 cm).

DEW
Liquid water that has condensed onto objects at or near the Earth's surface.

DEW POINT
The temperature at which water starts to condense out of a particular air mass.

DOWNBURST
A strong downdraft of fairly short duration that is produced by some thunderstorms.

DOWNDRAFT
An air current that is moving vertically downward.

DRIZZLE
Light rain consisting of drops smaller than 0.02 in (0.5 mm).

DROUGHT
Prolonged and abnormal shortage of water caused by lack of rainfall.

DUST BOWL
Area in the Great Plains region of the US, where extensive soil erosion occurred in the 1930s as the result of prolonged drought.

EVAPORATION
The process by which liquid water turns to water vapor and mixes with the air.

EVAPOTRANSPIRATION
The loss of water to the atmosphere as a result of the combined effect of evaporation and the transpiration of plants.

EXOSPHERE
The outermost layer of the Earth's atmosphere.

FOG
Water droplets in the air that reduce visibility to less than 1,100 yards (1,000 m).

FÖHN
The European term for a dry, downslope wind. *Also see* chinook.

FRONT
The boundary between two air masses.

FROST
White ice crystals deposited on the surface of objects that have a temperature below the freezing point of water.

HAIL
Pieces of hard, solid ice falling from clouds.

HAZE
Impaired visibility as a result of smoke, dust, or water vapor.

HEMISPHERE
One half of a sphere. The term is usually applied to regions north or south of the equator.

HIGH
See anticyclone.

HUMIDITY
The amount of water vapor in air.

HURRICANE
A powerful tropical storm with sustained wind speeds of more than 73 mph (118 km/h). Also known as a typhoon or cyclone.

HYGROMETER
An instrument for measuring humidity.

INVERSION
A reversal of the normal lapse rate of decreasing temperature with increasing altitude.

IONOSPHERE
A region of the upper atmosphere that reflects some radio waves.

ISOBAR
A line on a map or chart that links points of equal pressure.

JET STREAM
A strong, high-level wind that can reach speeds in excess of 200 mph (320 km/h).

LAPSE RATE
The rate at which air temperature decreases with increasing altitude.

LATITUDE
Position on the Earth's surface north or south of the equator.

LEE
The side of a mountain, hillside, or island that is facing away from the prevailing wind.

LIGHTNING
Discharge of static electricity in the atmosphere.

LONGITUDE
Position on the Earth's surface east or west of the Greenwich meridian.

LOW
See depression.

MESOSPHERE
The layer of the Earth's atmosphere above the stratosphere.

METEOROLOGIST
Someone who makes a scientific study of weather and weather

processes.

MILLIBAR
International unit for measuring air pressure, now sometimes called a hectopascal.

MIST
Slight impairment of visibility resulting from water droplets suspended in the air.

MONSOON
The seasonal shift in wind direction that brings alternate very wet and very dry seasons to India and much of Southeast Asia.

OROGRAPHIC RAINFALL
Enhanced rainfall as a result of moist air cooling as it is lifted up the side of a mountain range.

OZONE
A form of oxygen which has three atoms instead of the usual two. In the troposphere, ozone is a pollutant. In the stratosphere, ozone filters out harmful ultraviolet radiation.

PRECIPITATION
Water released from the atmosphere onto Earth's surface as rain, snow,

hail, dew, and fog.

RADIATION
Process by which energy can travel from a distant source.

RAIN
Drops of liquid water falling from clouds.

RAIN SHADOW
An area of decreased rainfall on the lee side of a hill or mountain.

REFRACTION
The bending of light as it passes from one medium to another, e.g., from air to water.

RIDGE
An elongated area of high air pressure.

SEA LEVEL
The normal level of high tide, used as a baseline for measuring height or depth.

SEEDER-FEEDER
The process of orographic rainfall by which high-level clouds "seed" rain clouds at a lower level.

SEEDING
The process by which condensation nuclei are artificially released into the atmosphere to encourage precipitation.

SIGWX
The abbreviation for Significant Weather Effects – weather that affects flying conditions.

SMOG
Dirty fog produced by air pollution in cities, and often occurring beneath a temperature inversion. The action of sunlight can produce photochemical smog.

SNOW
Ice crystals that fall from clouds and which may stick together to form snowflakes.

SNOWLINE
The vertical limit of snow lying on mountainsides throughout the year.

SNOWPACK
Snow lying on the ground for any significant period of time.

SOLSTICE
The time of year when the Sun appears to be directly overhead at either the tropic of Cancer or the tropic of Capricorn.

STRATOSPHERE
The layer of the Earth's atmosphere above the troposphere.

STREAMLINE
A line used on some weather maps to indicate wind flow.

SYNOPTIC CHART
A map that shows the weather conditions near the Earth's surface at a particular place and at a particular time.

THERMAL
A current of warm, rising air.

THERMOSPHERE
The layer of the Earth's atmosphere above the mesosphere.

THUNDER
The sound made by the expansion of air which has been heated by lightning.

TORNADO
A rapidly rotating low-pressure vortex that may form inside a storm cloud and reach down to the ground.

TREELINE
The vertical limit of tree growth on mountains.

TROPICS
The approximate area between two imaginary lines (the tropic of Cancer and the tropic of Capricorn) that encircle the Earth $23\frac{1}{2}°$ north and south of the equator.

TROPOPAUSE
The upper limit of the troposphere.

TROPOSPHERE
The innermost layer of the Earth's atmosphere, where most weather occurs.

TROUGH
An elongated area of low air pressure.

TSUNAMI
A destructive sea wave caused by an underwater earthquake or volcanic eruption.

TYPHOON
See hurricane.

UPCURRENT
An air current that is moving vertically upward.

WATERSPOUT
A tornado-like vortex that forms over water.

WIND
The horizontal movement of air from regions of high pressure to regions of low pressure.

Index

Acknowledgments

Dorling Kindersley would like to thank:

Hilary Bird for the index; Michael Dukes for invaluable assistance; and Stephen Johnson of International Computers Ltd, Manchester, the National Meteorological Office, London, Scientific American, Dr. M. Matson, and Dr. A. Roberts for reference material.

Illustrations by:

Peter Bull, Julia Cobbold, Richard Coombes, Brian Delf, Bill Donohoe, Mike Dunning, Roy Flookes, Mark Franklin, Mick Gillah, Mike Grey, John Hutchinson, Norman Lacey, Richard Lewis, Janos Marfy, Colin Rose, Colin Salmon, Mike Saunders, John Templeton, Alistair Wardle, John Woodcock, Martin Woodward.

The publisher would like to thank the following for their kind permission to reproduce the photographs:

Aeroports de Paris 119br; J. Allan Cash 85cl, 110tr, 117tr, 118tr, bc; Bruce Coleman Ltd/ Paul R. Wilkenson 10/11, Tor Oddvar Hansen 52tr, R.I.M. Campbell 53r, Jeff Foott Prod. 60tr, 75cr,106/107, Francisco J. Erize 61bl, Dr. Eckart Pott 67bl, Dr. Frieder Saver 66tr, John Shaw 67tl, Carol Hughes 75tl, Norman Tomalin 76/77, Hans Reinhard 86/87, Atlantide SDF 94tr, Eric Crichton 114tr; Ecoscene 40tr, Schaffer 148tr; ESA / ERS-1 47tl,140b,143tl, 143cr; Galaxy Picture Library 57b; Robert Harding Picture Library / J.H.C Wilson 22tr, 38tr; Heldref Publications/ Weatherwise Magazine 72tr, 75bl, 117cl; The Image Bank/ Bill Varie 149cr; F.L.P.A 56tr, 111bl, 116tr, Dembinsky 13tr, 55cl, S.Moody/Dembinsky 13cr; Silvestris 13br, 54tr, 114/115b; E.Tidman 21tl; W. Wisniewski 25tl; R.Wilmshurst 29tl; K.Nimmo 42tr; F.Folking 42tl; C.Carvalho 44/45, 64tr; E&D Hosking 74tr,95bl; D. Kinzler 96/97; H. Binz 100tr; R.Bird 101bl; D.Hoadley 102l; R.Steinau 103cl; J.C.Allen & Son 105bl, 146/147; National Meteorological Library /JFP Galvin 127cl, 110bl, br, 111tr, cl; NASA 12/13c, 62tr, 73tl, 90tr, 108tr, 141c, 141b,142; N.C.A.R 73br, 85br, 105cr, 117br, 119cl, 138tr, 141tl, 144tr, 145bl, bc, br; N.O.A.A. 41cr; Novosti 149bl; Oxford Scientific Films / David Fox 48tr; Panos Pictures /Neil Cooper 112tr; Pictor 98tr,113cl;R.K. Pilsbury 12l, 68/69, 70tr, 73cl, 137bl, 138b; Planet Earth / Richard Chester 103bl, Jerry Mason 134/135; Rex Features 50tr; Science Photo Library / Earth Satellite Corp 113tr, Jerry Mason 132tr, Peter Menzel 133bl, Hank Morgan 140tr, N.C.A.R 105tl, NRSC Ltd. 91tl, Pekka Parvianen 42bl; 57cl; P.Woicesshyn/NASA 143bl; 145cl; Tony Stone Images 118l; James Randkler 18/19, Greg Probst 58/59, Arnulf Husmo 62/63b, Hans Peter Merton 124tr; University of Dundee/ APEME 130tl, 131br; ZEFA / Hecker 81cr.